CEMETERY RECORDS OF GREENE C

ALABAMA AND RELATED AREAS

The Journal of Mrs. Mary Marshall

edited by

O'Levia Neil Wilson Wiese

Other Heritage Books from
O'Levia Neil Wilson Wiese:

The Woodville Republican, Volume 1
December 18, 1823 - December 17, 1839

The Woodville Republican, Volume 2
January 4, 1840 - October 30, 1847

The Woodville Republican, Volume 3
January 8, 1848 - January 9, 1855

A Facsimile Reprint

Published 1994 by

HERITAGE BOOKS, INC.
1540-E Pointer Ridge Place,
Bowie, Maryland 20716
(301) 390-7709

ISBN 1-55613-943-8

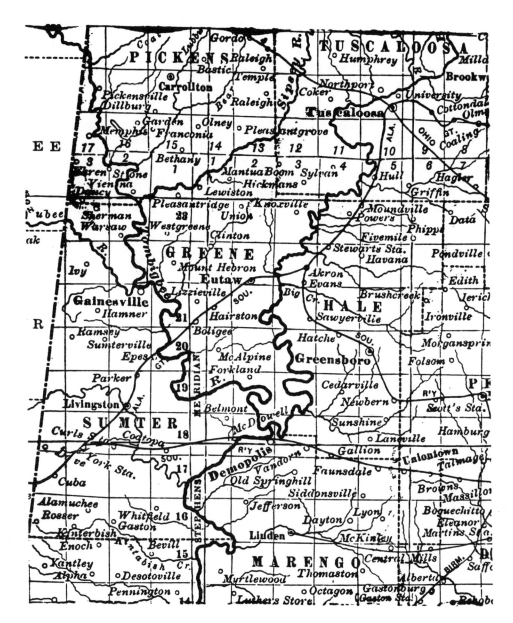

GREEN COUNTY

1897

INTRODUCTION

Mrs. Mary Marshall of Greene County Alabama has devoted much of her life researching the historical past of her community. At the time that I met her I had been researching my family less than ten years. I considered this meeting a miracle for I was deeply impressed with her experiences. Such was the case when three years ago I ventured into the community of Pleasant Ridge, Greene County Alabama searching for the "Old Discarded Bigbee Cemetery", and was directed to Mrs. Marshall's home.

This was truly a momentous occasion as she was able to share memories as well as facts about the country-side where my ancestors settled in 1822. Here, with their children, Brigadier General Joseph Hutton and his wife, Nancy Agnes Calhoun, immigrated from Edgefield District, South Carolina. Just a short time later, Joseph was buried in the Bigbee Cemetery. Many years have passed and today, saplings, briars and trees grow among as well as through the many graves that lie there. This is the fate of thousands of the old cemeteries of our ancestors and without diligent and dedicated people such a Mrs. Marshall, the ones who lie there would be forgotten.

This book, CEMETERY RECORDS OF GREENE COUNTY ALABAMA AND RELATED AREAS, contains complete as well as incomplete records of the various cemeteries. It is based on the journal of Mrs. Marshall and is not a record of my own research. If there are obvious errors in the editing of the material, remember that Waco, Texas is a long way from Greene County, Alabama, The asterisk has been used to designate her personal comments. In addition to these cemetery records, it is suggested that the reader refer to the GREENE COUNTY ALABAMA RECORDS, 1960, by Mrs. Marshall and Elizabeth Wood Thomas for further research in this area. Also a magnificent book, A GOODLY HERITAGE, MEMORIES OF GREENE COUNTY, 1977 by the Greene County Historical Society should not be overlooked.

OBSCURITY'S CRADLE

From the road I could see the foliage of the trees,
And I could hear the lulling sigh of the summer breeze.
The rusting iron gate was open, partially,
Enough for me, I walked into the ancient cemetery.

Sleep quietly, all who are here. Rest.
Nature has taken you to her breast.
Be comforted.
Be comforted.

There were no visitors, no one to clean
The grave, nor pull away the weeds between
The leaning stones. I looked in awe
At the moldering debris and disorder that I saw.
The roots of saplings, pines and oaks,
Grew through the graves. Each root-rope chokes
The coffin beds. Wandering winds carelessly blew
Broken branches and crumbling tombstones askew.

Sleep quietly, all who are here. Rest.
Nature has taken you to her breast.
Be comforted.
Be comforted.

These neglected dead were once our past.
Am I the only one who cares, at last?
Somewhere—somewhere descendents waste their prime
Forgetting these sleeping ones. Soon their time
Will come, and at nature's breast
They, too, will rest.
Be comforted.
Be comforted.

Lenora A. Gates

THE BIGBEE CEMETERY

". . . Let me watch the sun rise and set
With no pang or sad regret
For my own sun will set someday"

Garvin Germany

TABLE OF CONTENTS

Alabama Cemeteries

MISSISSIPPI CEMETERIES

BELMONT CEMETERY

Wayne C. Patton Sept. 29, 1826-Aug. 11, 1955

Annie L. Bates b. Oct. 6, 1818-Mar. 1865.

Wm. Bates Dec. 30, 1832-Dec. 16, 1853.
Elizabeth (Our Mother) d. May 17, 1844 aged 25
Wm. May Inf. son of T.B. and Eliz. May (Same tomb)

Wyatt Harper Oct. 15, 1799-Nov. 6, 1864.

Wyatt Judson Harper Oct. 9, 1835-July 8, 1858.

Mary Daisy wife of W. R. Dobson Nov. 4, 1870-June 29, 1892.

J.W. Harper oct 14, 1830-d. 1858.

Stephen Horton July 8, 1809-Oct. 18, 1888.

Elizabeth 2nd wife of Stephen Horton Oct. 8, 1811-Aug 25, 1886.

Frances S.A. Horton dau. of Stephen & E.A. Horton May 9, 1836-June 3, 1861.

Margaret Ann Horton dau. of S&E. A. Horton Oct. 6, 1844-Aug. 22, 1863.

J.Y. Grayson son of (Kiv ?? or Riv.) & S. E. Grayson Sept. 13, 1865-Nov. 26, 1865.

W. O. Grayson d. July 1867.

Sophie Harper b. Mar, 11, 1806-Feb. 7, 1863.

R.S. Harper Oct. 28, 1832-Aug. 24, 1895.

Wm. J. Harper Apr. 24, 1860-Apr. 17, 1911.

Shepherd Rushing Mar. 4, 1806-Feb. 17, 1885.

Ralph W. Grayson Aug. 4, 1840-Nov. 22, 1886.

Mollie Melton Davidson 1856-1893.

Sallie dau. of F. and M.M. Davidson Oct. 30, 1879-Aug. 20, 1882.

Rev. Bartlett Melton July 11, 1811-Oct. 24, 1856

Mary, wife of B. Melton d. Mar. 22, 1883-age 72.

C.C. Melton June 7, 1845-Nov. 27, 1900.

Ella Thomas Melton b. Aug. 24, 1861 at Butler Ala. d. May 23, 1917 Belmont.

Sallie E. Boyd 1862-1931.

Thomas W. Phares Jan. 13, 1871-July 6, 1892.

Father: William McKee d. Apr. 18, 1879 aged 71
Mother: Eliza C (or G) McKee d. Feb. 13, 1877 aged 57.

Z.C. Harper Dec. 6, 1848-Dec. 14, 1899.

Norma Wilson dau of W.J. and A.E. Harper. 1902-1903.

Davis Louis son of L. and M.A. Hadden Jan. 23, 1855 aged 18 months.

Stella dau of L. & M.A. Hadden July 14, 1857-Jan.22, 1863.

Sophia Elizabeth dau. of L. and M.A. Hadden Oct. 11, 1845-Oct. 22, 1848.

Vernon Tutt.W.O.W. 1875-1912.

Capt. James Tutt Co. C 8 Ala. CoU. CSA (Southern Cross of Honor).

John C. Perry b. N.C. 1791 d. Sumter Co. Ala 1815 aged 24
**(tomb says 26).

Adell Gillespie Feb. 1, 1851-d. 1852.

Marion Gillespie Oct. 29, 1846-June 13, 1847.

Capt. John W. Smith July 31, 1792-June 8, 1857.

Margaret Scott Smith Oct. 16, 1814-Sept. 6, 1840.

Josephine Smith

John W. Smith Jr.

Helen M. and John Henry wife and son of Dr. Frank Davidson.

Sins Blacksher Mar. 7, 1828-Nov. 2,1845.

Nancy wife of David Blacksher d. Jan. 19, 1851 age 55, 10 mo. 23 da.

David Blacksher Feb. 26, 1795-Oct. 17, 1868.

Wm. & Frances W. Blacksher.

Wm. d. Sept. 6, 1834 Frances Sept. 1840 age ?

Temperence wife of Hugh Blakeney June 23, 1816 d. Oct. 5, 1841.

Mary Rushing b. S.C. 1758 d. Ala. Aug. 22, 1837.

Winston, son of Leonidas & America E. Rushing d. 1859 aged 6 mo.

Elizabeth dau of James & Susan Rushing b. 1833.

Abner Evans Oct. 11, 1807-July 26, 1853.

Caldwell Estis d. Oct. 12, 1812 in 80th yr. (Born 1732).

Daniel Holyfield d. 1834 about 78 years.

James Rushing Nov. 8, 1846-Apr. 28, 1855.

Christopher C. son of J.M. & Susan Rushing Feb. 18, 1846-May 27, 1862.

Marshall B. son of J.M. & Susan Rushing Dec. 25, 1848- Jan 27, 1864.

Dr. W.W. Morgan Oct. 6, 1832-July 31, 1860.

James S. Tutt son of James V. & Sara P. Tutt. Nov. 21, 1851-Sept. 28, 1855.

Isabel wife of Dr. W.W. Morgan Oct. 6, 1832-July 31, 1860.

Oliver Moore McCurdy Nov. 14, 1807-May 11, 1844.

A.A. Powell Sept. 13, 1811-Oct. 2, 1875.

Penelope Powell d. Aug. 6, 1840 aged 20 yrs.

Temperance Powell July 29, 1814-Mar. 18, 1857.

Green Powell Jan. 10, 1802-1846 aged 44.

John Sheffield Ala. PVT CWS, W.W.I. June 10, 1891-June 18, 1952.

James F. Speed July 25, 1904-Apr: 26, 1946.

James T. Speed 1869-1926.

Origin W. Bates 1853-1933.

Mary Speed wife of O.W. Bates 1864-1935.

(Orignin W. Bates, Buster Gandy's grandfather)
Lou Ellen said Origin Bates=m= Jonnie Speed grandparents of Buster Gandy. Buster's mother Bertha Bates was their daughter =m= Aphis Omega Gandy.****

John M. Spidle Mar. 11, 1855-June 9, 1938.

Our Mother Sallie E. wife of John M. Spidle May 8, 1857-June 19,1921.

Jake Spidle 1881-1943.

Frances Spidle 1892.

Jacob Spidle Mar. 24, 1833-Sept. 18, 1885.

Harry L. son of J.M. and F. Spidle 1879-1882.

Elizabeth Spidle wife of Jacob Spidle Mar. 18, 1833-July 27, 1909.

John C. Phares 1881-1948.

Mabel K. Phares 1882.

James Raymond Phares Ala Pvt. ICL 330 Aug. 10, 1941.

John Murray son of Frank and Luka Richardson June 11, 1880-Oct. 2, 1884.

Carrie Richardson wife of W.T. Angelo Feb. 10, 1886-Sept. 30, 1905.

Inf. son Rawley Jan. 16, 1905-June 31, 1905.

Robert Spidle Apr. 15, 1863-Mar. 30, 1911.

WilliamSeibert Aug. 18, 1857-Nov. 16, 1889.

J. Nickel Seibert Feb. 21, 1813-Feb. 23, 1896.

Elizabeth wife of N. Seibert May 13, 1831-May 8, 1881.

John son of W. & E. Seibert d. Apr. 29, 1869, aged 20.

James B. Speed July 18, 1851-Sept. 9, 1878.

Bascom Melton May 13, 1849-Nov. 29, 1857.

Wm. L. Melton Nov. 1, 1835-May 18, 1854.

Sara J. dau of Lewis & Charlotte C. Henderson Oct. 24, 1829-Sept. 17, 1848.

Charlotte C. dau of Elijah and Sarah Curtis wife Lewis Henderson Sept 15, 1806-Apr. 19, 1845.

Elizabeth Jane dau.of Daniel G. Rencher Sept 10, 1843-aged 10 yrs. 11 mo.

C.C. wife of R.S. Harper Sept, 28,1838-May 26, 1860.

Eliza wife of Alexander Dallas Sr. b. Chesterfield S. C. Jan. 11, 1808-June 30, 1837.

Wm. Gaston son of Hugh & Elizabeth Jan. 10, 1832-Sept. 20, 1836.

Martha S. Arrington dau of West and Mary S. Arrington Sept. 25, 1834-Jan. 1, 1842.

Lucy McFarland wife of Dock Mills Taylor Aug 13, 1877-July 24, 1851.

Dock Mills Taylor Oct 22, 1865-June 10, 1938.

Octavia L. Taylor Oct 26, 1858-Oct 4, 1884
Madison B. Taylor May 28, 1863-Jan. 15, 1884.

G.B. Nuffer Mar. 1846- Aug. 7, 1874.
Nla Phillips Sept. 18, 1879-Sept. 18, 1895.

Buford Phillips Feb. 24, 1876-Nov. 3, 1898.

James Samuel Downing May 14, 1877-June 22, 1900

H.J. Phillips Dec. 12, 1844-Sept. 6, 1903.

Henry Jackson Phillips Oct. 17, 1839 - Aug.29, 1912

Judson J. son of N. & L. A. Hilman 1849-1871

M.S. Speed wife of J.B. Speed Dec.14, 1867- Dec.19, 1892

Lorenzo Rushing June 26, 1853 - Sept. 15, 1887

Laura Rushing 1886- 1892

Lewis Henderson 1807- Dec. 2, 1884 (Mason)

Obedience Henderson 2nd wife Lewis Henderson Mar. 10, 1910
Sept. 18, 1881

Adella M. dau. of O.E. and M. T. Smith Mar. 20, 1863- Sept. 20, 1881

Robert W. infant son of J.J. & L.E. Melton Aug. 18, 1884-Nov.9, 1885

Lizzie Speed May.31, 1853- Mar.10, 1893

Benjamin R. Speed Jan.11, 1826- Oct.18, 1866

Mrs. Mary McKee Gillespied d. Feb.19, 1859- aged 74

Sophia Munchief Feb.7, 1802- Oct.21, 1852

Sampson Munchief July 3, 1831- Mar.31, 1857

Frances M. Munchief d. Dec. 18, 1852- aged 16 yrs. 12 da.

Tempie B. Coats dau. of J.M. & Susan Rushing Jan. 11, 1842- Aug. 9, 1866

Susannah wife of J.M. Rushing b. N.C. 1810-1883

J.M. Rushing 1814-

American E. Rushing Aug. 21, 1834- Nov. 9, 1881

James Beazley Tutt Apr. 14, 1849- Mar. 27, 1913

Ada V. wife of James B. Tutt Apr. 5, 1851- Nov. 11, 1911

Wm. McAllister June 24, 1784- Dec. 14, 1853

Wm. F. son of Lewis & Charlotte C. Henderson Sept. 24, 1834- June 1, 1846

Lewis W. son of Lewis & Charlotte C. Henderson Apr. 11, 1832-Feb. 10, 1861.

Martha T. wife of C. E. Smith Feb. 10, 1840-May 28, 1866.

Mary Bettie dau. of U. T. and L. K. Blacksher Dec. 23, 1852-Jan. 27, 1857.

Cora Ella dau. of U. T. & E. K. Blacksher Oct. 11, 1848-Sept. 30, 1865.

Elizabeth K. 1st wife of U. T. Blacksher dau. of Joseph Patton Mar. 16, 1831-Oct. 4, 1861.

Constatine Perkins son of T. A. & N. E. Scales d. Aug. 29, 1863.

Mrs. Sara J. wife of R. W. Lawler dau. of Joseph Patton Feb. 23, 1835-Nov. 20, 1865.

James M. Hartsfield June 15, 1830-June 17, 1878.

Mabel Louisa & Ella Maude dau. of J. M & S. E. Hartsfield 1871-1878 1874-1878.

Wm. W. Little Dec. 25, 1877-Mar. 3, 1943.

Hiram G. Collins killed July 31, 1870 aged about 23

Job Meador b. Anson Co. N. C. Aug. 1, 1860-Feb. 28, 1867

Andrew Jackson Wimberly Feb. 28, 1860-Mar. 18, 1918

Cora Landrum Wimberly July 5, 1856-Mar. 18, 1918

Ernest Joel Wimberly Oct. 15, 1885-Aug. 22, 1954

George V. Vise Nov. 23, 1874-Mar. 11, 1930

Donna Turpin Vise Mar. 16, 1886-Feb. 22, 1927

Jane Flowers Vise Mar. 1, 1850-July 2, 1915

Wm. H. Vise (W. O. W.) Feb. 1, 1878-Jan 28, 1919

Mary Florence Flowers July 17, 1881-Aug. 11, 1902

Robert B. Flowers Jan. 11, 1848-May 5, 1913

Annie Cadwell wife of Robert B. Flowers Jan, 10, 1855- Apr. 15, 1921

Clyde Marshall son of M. C. & Florence B. Flowers Feb. 2, 1922-May 28, 1922

Inf. of M. C. & Florence July 8, 1923

Auneacy Nisbet July 19, 1894-Aug. 9, 1898

Anelia wife of John Z. Tutt Apr. 29, 1829-May 18, 1861

Inf. son of J. Z. & G. M. Tutt 1868

Dr. Stephen R. Cook husband of Eula Bell Cook Dec. 17, 1865-Feb. 26, 1910 **(W.O.W.)

Pamela E. George d. Dec.23,1895 age 33yr. 9 mo. 16 da.

W.R.Hatter Oct.26,1901 aged 34 yrs. 10 mo. 26 da.

Stephen R.Cook d. Jan.25,1867 aged 39.

Mary M. wife of Stephen R.Cook Apr.19,1880 aged 45.

R.H.Hatter

Katherine Hatter **(Katherine Hutton)

Col. John McKee Rockbridge Co. Va. b. 1771 died at "Hill Of Howth", Green Co.Ala.1833.
Agent of U.S. for Choctaw Indians. Member of Congress USA.

William Dunbar a native of Miss. Soldier of Confederate States. He died at "Hill of Howth".

Eliza P.Harding July 16,1862-1888
John Charles Chotard native of Miss. d. 1863. Soldier of CSA.

Col. J. I.Thornton 1824-1885

Wilkes C.MacLemore 1886-1911

Annie Burt MacLemore 1904-1911

James A.Anderson b. Spartanburg Dist. S.C. d. 1870 age 42

Dr. George G.Perrin b. Abbeville Dist. d. 1854 aged 48
(See Jarvis,Minor Blakely,Watson)

BEULAH CEMETERY
(Near Union)

Jesse F. Lyles Ala. Pvt. 313 Field Arty. 80 Civ. d. May 31, 1936 **(see Pooles, Hamiltons, Norris, Mayo, Sellars, Roebucks, Henderson)**

Capt. J.T. Smith wife Sara Dec. 1, 1829-Sept. 11, 1918

John A. Smith 1869-1939

Florence T. Smith 1870-1943

Geo. W. Lamb 1885-1937 Nanny C. 1888-1946

E. Kirby Smith Oct. 9, 1861-Sept. 30, 1887

D. Kimbrough Smith Apr. 13, 1864-Oct. 25, 1882

Rinie E. wife of J.M. Chambers 1853-1885

Luther S. Lamb 1878-1905

Josephine Hamilton wife of E.H. Lamb 1885

Florence Lamb wife of Oscar Spencer 1882-1936

Doris Spencer wife of Lyman Graham 1914-1939

Christie A. wife of M.B. Crawford 1880-1902

Martha wife of S.D. McGraw 1858-1883

Mary E. Smith Bonda 1871-1954

Martin Clay Bonds Sept. 30, 1852-Dec. 19, 1910

Annie Bonds 1893-1902

Robert Free d. 1881 aged 73 yrs. 11 mo. 16 da.

Simeon Free Nov. 20, 1811-Jan. 15, 1889

Eliza E. wife of Simeon Nov. 28, 1820-Oct. 1, 1901

E.T. Mabry 1836-1890

Robert E. Mabry 1872-1902

J. Matt Taylor 1875-1945

Ida Lamb Taylor 1876-1939

Mrs. L.M. Burnett 1819-1900

Fridelia Augusta wife of J.G. Bonds

E.W. Henderson 1847-1939

Nehemiah Cobb 1815-1888

David Cobb 1845-1863

Sara E. Chambers 1839-1865

James M. Chambers 1814-1864

Paschal P. Pearson 1852-1926

Lemuel T. Pearson 1862-1916

Rev. Albert M. Smith 1841-1877

Annie M. wife of Albert Smith 1844-1922

Marvin Reynolds 1835-1925

Margaret Drummond 1805-1875

Mary A. Richey 1831-1862

Rev. M.P. Smith 1805-1883

Martha E. his wife

Susan R. Smith 1823-1886

Luke Thornton 1795-1848

James Thornton 1835-1856

Capt. Peter Hamilton 1789-1850

Peter H. Hamilton 1818-1852

Mary A. wife of Capt. Peter Hamilton 1825-1900

Nancy C. Thornton 1832-1852 **(might be Nancy Griggs)
(M.R.H. Thornton)

Elisha Thornton 1792-1852

Mary Leatherwood Oct. 7, 1809-Sept. 23, 1859

Lydia P. Gillespie wife of John O(D) Gillespie d. 1842 age 53

Mary C. wife of W.W. Davis 1833-1857

Pinckney Phillips 1813-1886

Geo. Washington Smith

BIGBEE CEMETERY

Augustus G. son of J.M. and E.J. Hutton b. Sept. 23, 1841-Jan. 7, 1898(**Mrs. Hatter's brother)

Eliza Hutton b. Bibb Co. Ala. May 15, 1818 Greene Co. Ala. wife of Augustus Hutton

John N. (Newton) Hutton b. Abbeville Dist. S.C. June 3, 1807 D. Greene Dec. 11, 1877

John A. son of John N. & Eliza J. Hutton. b. Aug. 24, 1849-June 30, 1852.

Sallie A. Hutton Hatter 1848-1926

Richard N. Hatter 1871-1926

Geo. Hill son of John S. and Della McGowin b. July 26, 1869-Jan. 17, 1870

IN AN IRON FENCE ENCLOSURE

David H. Williams M.D. Oct. 25, 1827-Feb. 3, 1907
Eugenia Floride Williams b. Hopewells Greene Co. (**P.O. in 1854) Ala. Feb. 4, 1832 d. Gainesville Mar. 2, 1910

Clarence Williams b. Feb. 6, D. Dec. 17, 1865 2nd son of Dr. D.H. and E.F. Williams

Little Benji and Little Bessie

Aquilla D. Hutton M.D. b. Abbeville Dist. S.C. Apr. 8, 1805 d. Greene Co. Ala. Dec. 6, 1852

Mrs.Elizabeth H. Hutton b. July 22, 1813 Edgefield Dist. S.C. (**born Tutt) Married Feb. 2, 1831 to Aquilla D. Hutton M.D. d. Feb. 1, 1854.

Joseph A. Hutton died from diarrhea Oct. 10, 1850 b. Oct. 15, 1833.

Alonzo Hutton 2nd son of A.D. & E.H. Hutton

Cornelia Adon 2nd dau. b. Apr. 18, 1838 died of congestive fever Sept. 1, 1842

John R. son of G.M. and Elizabeth Trantham. June 27, 1818-Sept. 19, 1826

Frances Wilkes d. 1834 age 66 b. about 1768.

Mary Wilkes 1843 age 64 b. about 1779

Our Emmett son of R.F. and M.A. Stuart age 5.

Martha Dirrut dau. of J. and M.T. Greer aged 2

James Francis son of J. and M.T. Greer aged 2

Wm. H.H. Stone native of Greenville Dist. S.C. son of Banister Stone b. Mar. 13, 1814 d. July 14, 1835 in 22nd yr.

(**Martha Dirrut White)

Alexander Thompson native of S.C. Feb. 6, 1774-Oct. 18, 1848 (**near Wilkes)

Elethe (**or Alettia in 1850 census) Ann wife of Wm. F. Bell and dau. of Andrew and Sophie Brownlee b. in Lowndes Co. Miss. July 10, 1830-Sept. 29, 1850.

Sophia Brownlee wife of Andrew Brownlee b. 1810-d. May 4, 1852.

William S. Brownlee son of Andrew and Sophia Brownlee b. 1839 d. 1849.

Mrs. Mary Kirkland Mar. 26, 1844 age 70 yrs. 6 mo. 4 da.

Clizabeth B. consort of Dr. Burrell Huggins dau. of Isaac and Mary Kirkland.

Amos Tims b. Chester Dist. S. C. b. Aug. 31, 1771 d. Pickens Co. Dec. 29, 1867

Mary Finns dau. of Thomas L. and Elly Cabeen b. Aug. 1777 d. Nov. 29, 1824

Robert Craig b. June 28, 1800 d. Oct. 18, 1860

Catherine C. Craig wife of Robert Craig. Feb. 18, 1797-July 8, 1856 (**One James Craig settled in Athens Ala. about 1800)

Cornelia Jane Craig dau. of Robert and Catherine Craig Nov. 23, 1829-Oct. 23, 1831

James Newton Craig. son of R. & C. C. Craig May 24, 1837-Oct. 13, 1841

Augusta Dwan Craig dau. of Robert & Catherine Craig June 1, 1834-Sept. 20, 1842

Marcellus Octabius Craig. b. Mar. 19, 1832-Sept. 1, 1842 son of Robert and Catherine Craig

Gen. Joseph Hutton d. Aug. 30, 1823 of Cholera Morbus age 56
**He married Nancy Calhoun 1st cousin of stateman John C. Calhoun & consort of Gen. Joseph Hutton, died after a few days illness with congestive fever. age 67.
(Note:
The above statement by Mrs. Marshall is only a part of the tomb information. Also, the grave of Nancy Agnes Calhoun daughter of William and Agnes Long Cahoun is at the foot of her husband. In 1978, my husband and I found her headstone under eight inches of

silt and debris. Today, it rest beside her husbands headstone. His tomb reads as follows: Sacred to the memory of Gen'l Joseph Hutton: who departed this life after a few days illness from Cholera Morbus on the 30th of Aug. 1823 aged 53 yrs. 8 mo. 2 days. He immigrated from S. Carolina Abbeville Dist. to this State in April 1822. He was for several years prior to his death an exemplary member of the Presbyterian Church Vale! Vale!

Her tomb reads as follows:
Sacred to the memory of Mrs. Nancy, Consort of Gen'l Joseph Hutton, who departed this life after a few days illness of congestive fever on the 5th of Sept. 1840, aged 67 years & 8 days. She was for many years before her death, an exemplary member of the Presbyterian Church.

"How blest the righteous when they die!
When sinless a weary soul to rest
How mildly beam the closing eyes
How gently heaves the expiring breast"

Mary H. Tilman wife of D. W. Tilman b. Apr. 28, 1800-May 30, 1824. (Mary was sister of Joseph Hutton)

Tomb reads as follows: Mary H. Tilman, wife of D. W. Tilman born April 28, 1800, Died May 30, 1824, aged 24 years.
"Rest sweet Mother, Jesus took thee, We shall greet thee here no more. He sent an Angel Safe to waft thee To a brighter, better shore"

Dan W. Tilman husband of Melissa Tilman b. Union Dist. S. C. July 19, 1800-Nov. 10, 1830

Tomb reads as follows: In memory of Dan W. Tilman, husband of Melissa Tilman, born in Union district. S. C. July 19, 1800, and departed this life, Nov. 10th 1830.
"Thou art at rest where storms can vex no more,
When shall we meet again and kiss away
The tears of joy in one eternal day"

Mrs. Justinia Va. Clanton Dec. 4, 1839-Mar. 20, 1857

John Moore Hill b. Feb. 22, 1843-Feb. 18, 1853

William Judge Hill Jan. 19, 1837-Nov. 30, 1845

Mrs. Rebecca S. Saunders Feb. 22, 1821-Jan. 9, 1894

Thomas Jefferson Hill Aug. 6, 1834-July 10, 1853

Inf. son May 23, 1848-Dec. 30, 1848. Children of Geo. W. and Sara A. Hill (**connected with Nathaniel Greene

Sevilla N. Hill Sevilla Roden d. July 23, 1844 b. ca 1759 86 yrs. of age Widow of Moses Hill Edq. who died in Fairfield District S. C. July 1, 1821 in 63rd yr. b. 1758

Martha A. Pearson wife of Moses H. Pearson b. Dec. 29, 1828-Mar. 19, 1848 (**Jolly, I think)

Mary Thompson wife of Alexander Thompson d. Feb. 1842 aged 67

Mrs. Sara R. Hill d. Dec. 23, 1864

Rebecca C. Hill wife of Dr. T. De Graffenried b. Dec. 20, 1807 married to Dr. Mar 25, 1828 and died of billious fever Aug. 11, 1842 leaving a fond and affectionate husband, 3 sons and an infant daughter. She was daughter of Moses Hill Esq. of Fairfield dist. S. C. member of Methodist church for nearly 20 years and died in peace.

Celestia F. S. dau. of Dr. T. DeGraffenreid b. Mar. 26, 1839-Aug. 12, 1842

Rebecca H. dau. of Dr. T. DeGraffenreid b. Feb. 25, 1833-Aug. 15, 1842 of billious fever

Elizabeth A. DeGraffenreid third and last of Dr. DeGraffenreid Aug. 23, 1841-died of Rheumatism of the heart July 16, 1857

John Calhoun son of John F. and Anne Eliza DeGraffenried b. July 2, 1852-Apr. 26, 1854

Christopher M. son of J. F. and A. E. DeGraffenreid Nov. 1, 1856-Sept. 19, 1857

Trezevant son of J. F. and A. E. DeGraffenreid b. Dec. 4, 1858-Apr. 22, 1859

John F. DeGraffenreid buried at Pleasant Ridge Mar. 8, 1831-Apr. 21, 1886

Aquilla H. Coleman son of Charles H. and Pricilla A. (**Hutton) Coleman Sept. 8, 1831-Dec. 7, 1857

Priscilla Ann wife of Chas. H. Coleman b. Abbeville Dist. S. C. Dec. 27, 1809-Dec. 11, 1863 in Greene Co. (**Priscilla Hutton I think)

Agustus Coleman son of Chas. H. & Priscilla

Harveys White

Laura A. E. White (**John White's Mother) (John White owned old Will Hardy Home**)

Della Street Sept. 6, 1796-Mar. 22, 1851

Julia Ann Street Jan. 22, 1850-July 15, 1850

Wm. B. Wills erected by his wife E. M. W. d. June 20, 1840 of gunshot wounds. Oral will.

Wm. Rutledge Aug. 7, 1843 aged 4 yrs. 2 mo. b. about 1839

Isaac Rutledge b. ca 1811

Mary Kirkland

Mattie Kirkland

James Wills (Forkland) 32 KY b. about 1818 b. 1840 (**son James)

(**Aunt Laura Rutledge b. ca 1846 (4 in 1850)

William Bryan son of T. and Catherine C. Bryan 1827-1830

W. L. Brown 1802-1821

Bryant Bizzelle son of James & Patience Bizzelle b. Duplin Co. N. C. Apr. 26, 1829 died in Sumter Feb. 26, 1851 age 21 yrs. 10 mo.

Elizabethe Bizzelle dau. of James & Patience Bizzelle b. 1827-1848

James Bizzelle 1802-1844

Elisha H. Bryan 1820-1842

James G. George D. Feb. 10, 1831 aged 59 yrs. ca 1772

Nancy Wilmouth dau. of James G. & Permela E. George b. Aug. 5, 1840-Feb. 26, 1845

Catherine C. Hutton m. Wm. T. Bryan then married Robert Craig in 1839 (Wm. T. Bryan b. S. C. 1799 d. Aug. 1827 Stokes Cemetery Greene Co. Came to Green 1820)

William Bryan son of Wm. T. and Catherine C. Bryan b. Nov. 6, 1827-Jan 27, 1830

James C. son of James George & Permela Hutton Jan. 16, 1842-Sept. 7, 1846

BOLIGEE CITY CEMETERY
Greene Co. Ala.

Thomas Sterling Hylton apr. 5, 1844-Mar. 13, 1925 A Confederate soldier 21st Ala. Witherspoon Guards Drummer Boy of Shiloh

Louis Marion Grauer Mar. 25, 1859-Mar. 10, 1952

Daisy Hylton Grauer Nov. 1, 1872-Nov. 16, 1953

Hylton Warren Grauer son L.M. and D.H. Grauer Aug. 8, 1895-Dec. 31, 1920

Eliza Perry Minor May 19, 1842-June 19, 1917

Rosa Sanford Dandridge Jan. 12, 1856-Jan. 29, 1932

Mary Arrington wife of Samuel Harrison Johnston July 27, 1854-Nov. 18, 1917

Samuel Harrison Johnston b. Boligee Dec. 8, 1840-d. Jan. 24, 1915 Confederate Vet. Co. G. 1nd Ala. Cavalry 2nd Lieut.

William Willoughby "C. E. Rens" 1898-1936

Dr. P. B. Minor b. Jan. 22, 1828-June 26, 1884

John Fant Demoville Apr. 19, 1895-Mar. 29, 1955

A. B. Demoville Aug. 29, 1865-May 2, 1927

Isora Glover Demoville Dec. 20, 1867-Apr. 9, 1952

Bettie Jackson Pritchett wife of James Pritchett Dec. 10, 1854-Feb. 5, 1924

James Pritchett Mar. 25, 1851-Dec. 8, 1944

Sara Pritchett McAlpine Oct. 15, 1888-July 24, 1957

Mary Ridgeway McAlpine Aug. 26, 1850-May 6, 1920

Winston McAlpine 1904-1923

Julia McLenmore wife of Henry T. Bouchelle Jr. Dec. 18, 1890-Sept. 13, 1935

Maria Barbour Bauchelle July 25, 1847-Dec. 18, 1920 **I think dau. of Philip F. Barbour

Bradley Ridgeway McAlpine Nov. 18, 1875-Apr. 8, 1922

Delia Frances Bouchelle wife of Wilmen Payner b. 1887-1909

Henry Tutwiler Bouchelle Apr. 25, 1863-Mar. 9, 1913

Innes Brown Gould wife of Henry Tutwiler Bouchelle Apr. 2, 1866-Mar. 27, 1956

Ezra Fisk Bouchelle b. 1803

Blanch Shattuck 1808-1904

Samuel Joseph Burch June 27, 1877 d. Jan. 29, 1939

Philip Barbour Minor Dec. 15, 1875-Sept. 14, 1922

Hattie A. wife of S. A. Barnett Oct. 1844-Nov. 1901

Dr. John L. Minor d. Sept. 27, 1892 aged 29

L. B. Smaw Aug. 13, 1814-Dec. 24, 1894

Annie R. wife of L. B. Smaw Dec. 27, 1820-Dec. 22, 1899

Guy Pendleton Brugh 1876-1926

T. C. Hawkins b. Due West S. C. 1823-1908

Annie Thornton Byrd **Byrds & Means

Delia Thornton Means

John David Means Apr. 20, 1847-Dec. 7, 1891 A soldier of Confederate States.

Delia Francis, wife of Capt. John McKee Gould b. Apr. 3, 1831-Feb. 19, 1905 Soldier of Confederate States Inspector General Pettus Brigade Army of Tenn. Port Gibson, Baker's Creed, Vicksburg, Missionary Ridge, Lookout Mountain, Dalton to Atlanta, wounded at Duck River Tenn. 1864 Surrendered with Army at Salisbury N. C. Apr. 26, 1864

Catherine Marshall Byrd 1890-1911

Catherine Marshall Byrd dau. of J. McKee Gould and Delia Gould Apr. 23, 1861-Feb. 7, 1891

Matie H. Harlan 1860-1890 **Byrd Lot

Lyda Means wife of J. L. Beech Sept. 9, 1888-Oct. 28, 1918 Mother and Inf. decd.

Daniel Hall Trice June 30, 1872-Nov. 12, 1954

Daniel Hall Trice Jr. 1912-1919

Samuel Thetford M. D. 1878-1947

John McKee Gould July 4, 1846- July 24, 1945

Jeanie Huldah Mar. 24, 1868 - May 14, 1955

Susie Perry Byrd **Mr. Taylor Byrd's wife. Mar. 5, 1878 Nov. 25, 1951

Annie Baskin Harkess wife of Joseph W. Perry Jan. 29, 1863 at Clinton d. Oct. 5, 1915 at Lake City, Fla.

Josephine Whittaker dau of Joseph W. and Annie B. Perry Oct. 13, 1900- Jan. 27, 1905

Joseph Whittaker Perry b. Franklin Co. N.C. Feb. 20, 1845-d. Boligee, Feb. 14, 1902

Daniel H. Byrd Pvt. 2nd Ala. Inf. Spanish-American War. June 9, 1876-July 30, 1951**Youngst brother of Taylor Byrd the Caretaker.

Eliza Cothard Perry wife of Joseph W. Perry dau. of J. McKee and Delia Gould 1856-1895

Fannie Leslie dau. of R.H. Leslie d. Jan. 15, 1904**See Leslie's Shady Grove

Martha E. Pickel May 2, 1845- Aug. 5, 1912

J.C. Pickel husband of Martha E. Pickel b. Dec. 18, 1813- May 1, 1902

FORDS AND MARSHALLS

Annie Mary Ford d. Oct. 20, 1918 m. Apr. 1, 1899 in Atlanta

S.M. Marshall b. July 25, 1875 d. Oct. 19, 1957

Elinor Ford Marshall b. June 6, 1902 d. June 10, 1902

Mary Ford Marshall b. Apr. 12, 1905 d. Apr. 12, 1905

Martha E. Marshall b. Apr. 26, 1908

Mildred Mae Marshall b. Mar. 28, 1912

Samuel Marvin Marshall Jr. Mar. 24, 1914- Oct. 21, 1920
Lucille Ann Marshall Nov. 2, 1915

COLVIN CEMETERY

NEAR MRS. HERBERT GOSA NEAR UNION
**Jimmie and I went July 1960

John G. Brown Feb. 18, 1851-Nov. 10, 1870

Sinthey E. dau. of Thomas and Elizabeth Colvin Feb. 9, 1835-Dec. 22, 1839

Francis M. Colvin son of Thomas and Elizabeth Colvin July 26, 1825-Aug. 16, 1862

Thomas Colvin Dec. 11, 1797-Feb. 22, 1871

Elizabeth Colvin Dec. 15, 1802-Jan. 5, 1872

Thomas Colvin son of A. Rand & Savilla Davis July 8, 1849-Nov. 6, 1854

Eula Lee dau. of Dr. J.J. and Annie Smith Jan. 7, 1875-Mar. 1, 1877

**John G. Brown m. Elizabeth M. Colvin in Greene 1849 C-1 20

Nehemiah Cabb (Cobb) m. Mary Colvin 1843 B-316

**Old Ebeneezer Church where my mother joined when a little girl.

Julia V. wife of Dr. Gabriel m. Baker. b. Aug. 1834 d. Apr. 4, 1881.

Robert Marshall b. Coventry Warwickshire, England, 1811 d. 1880.

Margaret McDow d. July 9,1846 in 81st yr.

Arthur McDow May 20,1839 in 84th year.

Sander's Walker d. Jan.20.1865 aged 66yr. 5mo.
circa 1798 or 1799

Thomas Brandon Kennedy b. ca. 1772 d. June 24, 1858 in 86th year.

Elizabeth M. Kennedy d. Aug. 18, 1848 in 74 year (Circa 1774)

(this name was crossed out-Wiese) and M. Jane Cochrane.

Charles D. Stalworth son of Sahra E. and William Stalworth b. mar 9,1863 d. Aug.1,1865

Nancy Jane Harris b. June 10, 1824 d. Feb. 14, 1908

Sara T. Miller wife of Chas. H. Miller b. May 20, 1804 d. Aug. 31, 1882

Charles H. Miller b. Oct. 11, 1793 d. July 11, 1876

Jocob Lockhart Husband of Matilda Lockhart Jan. 7, 1828-Feb. 5, 1899

Mary S. Strait (**former Mary S. Boyd, my great-grandmother) b. Dec. 2, 1808 d. Nov 5, 1861 (**John died Feb. 9, 1857)
(John Strait married Mary S. Boyd in S. C. Feb. 5, 1829 Orphans court, est. book s-315. Final of Johns estate. Grandmother Grantham Eliz. b. May 20, 1824 d. Aug. 24, 1894.)**

John Strait (**my great grandfather) b. Dec. 8, 1806 d. Feb. 9, 1857.

Samuel W. Strait wife Fannie Strait b. Apr. 17, 1840, d. Dec. 18, 1893

S. T. Shaw b. Aug 10, 1855 d. Mar. 21, 1923.

Mary Helen wife of S. T. Shaw b. May 10, 1862 d. Oct. 29, 1909 dau. of James and Eliza Strait. The former Eliza Moten. James Strait brother of John Strait.

Eliza wife of James Strait d. Apr. 18, 1896 aged 70. James Strait died while on a visit back to Chester Dist. S. C. and was buried there.

James A. son of James and Eliza Shait b. Oct. 4, 1860 d. Dec. 15, 1885

Walter Scott son of James and Eliza Shait 1852-1856

Margaret Shait b. June 3,1770 d. Dec. 2,1839

Christopher Strait b. Aug 30,1840 d. Sep. 26,1840

Caroline E. Milner wife of J. S. Milner d. May 5, 1853

Children of Nathaniel and Elizabeth Birchett.

Furniford and Louisa Strother.

James Ed Milner 1812–1877

Frances Mabry

John P. Freeman Jr.

John P. Freeman 1822–1858

Patty J. Freeman 1854–1863

Wife of French S. Goodlaw 1812–1863

Elizabeth M. Coleman b. July 21, 1825 d. May 9, 1852

**(Jessie B.W. Coleman 1821–1840
Enos Amason Nash Co.N.C.d. 1876 Mason
Eliz Amason b. N.C. 1818–1898)**

William Coleman Mar. 20,1872 Sept. 20,1844

Nancy A. Coleman 1828–1848

Wm E. Jones b. S.C. Jan 10,1820 aged 51

WM Gass of Penn died 1817 at 37

Lavinia Jordan Wilson Sept. 4, 1839-Aug. 5,1938

Robert B. Wilson son of Cephas Love and Emily Beverly Wilson July 4, 1868-Mar. 6, 1889

Cepas Love Wilson son of Cepas Love and Emily Beverly Wilson Nov. 1846

Cepas Love Wilson son of Cepas Love and Della Mariah Wilson b. May 3, 1871 m. Louise Roebuck d.-----

Robert Bullington Wilson son of Cepas Love & Della Mariah Wilson Aug. 1, 1879 m. Margaret Norwood

Daughter Della Mariah m. Stephen E. Nash

Stanton Nash b. Nov. 11, 1852 (**Tom Payner has old Mooring family Bible)

F. G. Mooring to his wife Julia A. Mooring **(Moorings in Gainsville Cemetery. I think Julia Mooring was a Stanton)

Our parents-S. H. and H. J. Sanders d. Dec. 14, 1896 & Jan. 11, 1887 aged 63 & 66 (Hany's folks)

James P. Dunlap wife Annie E. May 22, 1842-July 10, 1855

Sallie Clara, wife of Rev. L. S. Hanley May 5, 1846-May 1, 1773

Leonidas Hutton b. Mar. 20, 1833 Greene Co. son of Wm. J. and Ann Hutton 29th Ala. Regt. d. Aug. 6, 1864 Griffin Ga. Burried there

Wm. Josephus Hutton son of James (correction Joseph) & Nancy Calhoun Hutton b. Affeville Dist. S. C. Oct. 21, 1802 moved to Greene 1822 died May 12, 1862-20

Kate wife of W. R. B. Hatter d. May 28, 1867 age 21

Eliza wife of J. R. Carpenter d. July 15, 1848 age 39

Mary Spidle wife of John M. Spidle Oct. 27, 1869 age 38

Thomas Daugherty Co. Tyrone Ireland Jan. 25, 1820-Aug. 13, 1884

Isabella dau. of Wm. W. & Pherebe Paschall b. July 14, 1840 d. Jan. 13, 1858

James Roddy Hall May 22, 1785-Sept. 23, 1849

Wife Rebecca Hall d. Nov. 26, 1865 age 75

Maj. Geo. Higginbolteam Amherst Co. Va. July 5, 1791-May 6, 1859

Capt. S. W. McAliley Cluster S. C. Sept. 24, 1836-Jan. 28, 1888

Wm. H. Pippen July 6, 1823-Feb. 21 1889

Wife Belle or Bettie June 10, 1846-Feb. 25, 1894

Anna S. Gordon Apr. 16, 1854-July 27, 1889 **(Nancy Medora Stelles's sister)**

Inf son of R. B. and F. S. Gordon July 20, 1889

Martha Dunlap wife of Robt. Dunlap & dau. of Arnals & J. W. Jolly

Mollie E. Cook wife of S.C. Brown Sept. 25,1840–Sept. 28,1909

J. and M. Jane Cochrane dau Mary Georgia d. Oct. 30,1853 age 14 mo. 15 da.

Laura E. Cook Nov. 9,1911

Sarah T. Miller wife of Charles Miller May 20, 1808-Aug. 31, 1882.

John J. Miller b. 1830–d. Nov. 19,1866.

James Gill b. Apr. 14,1760–Apr. 14,1842

Mary A. Gill b. June 1775-Nov. 27, 1850

John Thompson b. 1853- 1862 (this was crossed out but could be read)
Also Mrs. Marshall had: Shait son James & Eliza.
Samuel W. Strait, brother of John Strait m. Nancy Gill had dau. Mary Elizabeth Strait.
Robert Gill son of James & Mary A. Gill (Samuel W. Strait & Nancy Gill m. Dec. 19, 1832)**

Mary E. Strait m. Thos. H. Rogers July 8, 1869

Anne E. wife of T.J. Gordon Mar. 22, 1840-Aug 17, 1885

Chas E. son of Annie E. & T.J. Gordon

Edward E. Gordon Dec. 20, 1873-Apr. 6, 1932 Mason (Rhiney 1st teacher)***

Harry W. son of Wm.H. & Kate G. Miller 1886-1906

Chas M. Barry b. Eutaw Jan. 4, 1777

Jane Barry consort of Chas M. Barry d. Aug. 31, 1856 age 64

Lizzie J. Barry d. Mar. 9, 1956 age 64

Margaret Barry 1844

James Breathwaite Dublin Ireland Hambag Co.

Peter Burns d. May 22, 1851 (**James Strait m. his widow)**Maude's grandfather**)

Mrs. B.W. Brown wife of W.W. Brown 1808-1881

Wm. Davitt

Col. Simeon Maxwell wife Elizabeth Mar. 19, 1801 Nov. 22, 1866

Simeon & Elizabeth Maxwell Mar. 28, 1840 Oct. 5, 1859

Josephine Isabella dau. Simen & Eliz. Lucien m. son of Christopher & Te?? Shaw b. May 5, 1860-Feb. 11, 1884

S.C. & M.E. Brown Stephen C. & Mollie E.

Mary T. wife of James B. Cook Dec. 1836-Feb. 1871

Virginia Anderson Thomas Dec. 16, 1829-June 30, 1871

Sallie Higginbotham wife of Major Geo. G. Higginbotham dau. of Benjamin & Elizabeth Fortson b. Elbert Co. Ga. Mar. 30, 1800 **(Elijah Fortson m. Elizabeth Richard dau. of Wm. Richard Book I)**

Rev. J.R. Webster b. Shelby Co. Ala. Dec. 6, 1827 d. Jan. 12, 1860 Ordained to Ministry May 16, 1857 m. Apr. 28, 1858.

William W. Stallworth

wife Sara E. Clinton 1824-1908

Fanny Gordon Apr. 16, 1854 July 27, 1889

Mary A. wife of Robert O. Hunter d. orb. 1837

Carrie Lee dau. F.B. & R.L. Tarr Jan. 6, 1873 July 8, 1888

Mary Va. Richardson wife of Benj. T. Higginbotham Oct. 6, 1831-Mar. 7, 1853

Mary Ann Pettigrew

John Dunlap. Elizabeth Dunlap 1795-1869

CONCORD CEMETERY
1816

Elizabeth Skinner wife of E. W. Hardy 1853-1917

Wm. C. Otey Notloway (Nottoway?) Co. Va. d. 1842-age 26

Samuel J. Wilson Williamsburg Dist. S.C. May 16, 1790
Sept. 17, 1844. Cross in honor of Service War of 1812

Mary E. dau. of Samuel J. & Elizabeth K. Wilson Dec. 20, 1843-June 2, 1815

Samuel A. Wilson 1820-1875

Mrs. Mary E. Wilson 1831-1902

James Ezra Wilson Mar. 4, 1835-June 9, 1884

Frank Summer son of L. W. and M. J. Winn b. 1890-1896

James Jack Cooke

James Jack May 7, 1800-Dec. 27, 1875

Mary Julia Witherspoon 2nd wife of James Jack 1821-1890

Wm. M. Wilson 1824-18?2

Sara Wilson 1828-1898

Capt. Chas. Stewart Feb. 25, 1812 **(see Tucker Stewart) Nov. 17, 1893.

Mattie J. Stewart Jan 10, 1853-Aug. 8, 1890

James Brantly d. Nov. 4, 1862-age 72

William Wallace Borden Sept. 30, 1845-Apr. 22, 1898

Mary T. Borden wife of W. W. Borden Nov. 16, 1846-Dec. 22, 1908

Mary Leila Borden wife of S. F. Harry Jan. 14, 1881-July 18, 1903

Inf. dau J. F. and E. D. Bishop

James Simmons son of Alexander and Sara Pearre b. Columbia county Ga. Dec. 8, 1830 died Apr. 6, 1851

Martha Alice dau of James and E.J. Jones b. Greene Co. Jan. 16, 1854 died Nov. 9, 1866

Rhoda Simmons dau of James & Eliz. J. Jones

Alexander Pearre b. Augusta, Ga. May 25, 1799-d. June 6, 1858

John Randolph Jones b. Greene June 11, 1830 died Brownsville Tex. Feb. 18, 1861 age 30.

James Jones b. Columbia Co. Ga. Jan. 27, 1800 d. Hale Co. Apr. 29, 1880 age 80 yrs. 3 mo. "An honest man the noblest work of God."

Elizabeth Jane Pearre wife of James Jones Mar. 27, 1826-May 18, 1899

John O.A. Pearre son of Alexander & Sara Pearre b. Columbia Co. Ga.

Dr. John Calvin Wilson 1828-1892

Susan A. Jones wife of Dr. John C. Wilson 1837-1901

Evelyn Wilson wife of N.T. Richmand dau of J.C. & S.A. Wilson

H. Lee Brown Sr. Feb. 7, 1861-Dec. 9, 1927

Laura Irene wife 1864-1901

Robert Jones son of Wm. Jones Columbia Co. Ga. d. June 11, 1810 age 16 yr. 7 mo. 5 days.

Wm. M. Jones

Thomas Francis son of Robert & S.H. McKennie 1831-1847

Leah & J.F. Davis

James P. Powers b. Edgefield Co. S.C. Feb.1, 1829-Feb. 5, 1886

Julia Wilson Powers 1841-1906

Lewis G. Wilson b. May 19, 1837-Jan. 24, 1895

Margaret Nesmith b. Ireland near Belfast Jan. 20, 1784

Sara Florella Wilson

David Wilson d. 1873 age 81

John Whitney son of J.W. & S.A. Flemming Sept. 11, 1852-died Sept. 16, 1857 age 5

Mary Selma Wilson dau of Sara and David Wilson b. 1833-1851

Lawrence Richard inf son of Robert K. Kennedy & Maude Heddleston

Patrick Haustan son of James & Ann S. Jack Dec. 6, 1829-Aug. 10, 1858 (Houston??)

Simeon Glenn July 30, 1835 age 45

Mrs. Mildred Travis and Enoch Travis

Dr. James S. Fulton Sept. 22, 1820-Apr. 27, 1901

Wife Louisa M. May 5, 1825-Feb. 6, 1895 dau of Simeon & Nancy Glenn d. 1835

Martha Lenora dau of Alexander & Sara Pearre Columbia Co. Ga. Nov. 7, 1838-Feb. 20, 1836

Ann S. Jack 1st wife of James Jack **(1821-1890)** born Jan. 2, 1803 d. Apr. 16, 1888

Hugh Lavendar Ala. Pvt. S.C. Troops   Rev. War 1754-1834

James Brantley d. Mar. 15, 1880 age 89 yrs. 4 mo.

Pinckney Rice 1810-1857

Susannah Hutchensson wife of Robt. McKeemie 1789-1864

Mary Stephenson b. Oct. 26, 1789 d. Mar. 9, 1824

Major E.D. Whitehead b. Nash Co. N.C. born Oct. 15, 1797

Rebecca Whitehead d. Nov. 14, 1861 in 84th yr.

Albert Pinckney Whitehead b. Nash Co. N.C. Nov. 27, 1823 d. May 2, 1846 son of E.D. and Rebecca Whitehead

W.C. Sorshy b. Nash Co. N.C. Dec. 9, 1812 d. Dec. 1, 1853 buried in Whitehead lot.**(Related to Jennson Real Estate B'ham.)

Stephen Sorshy born Nash Co. N.C. Oct. 14, 1809 d. Mar. 17, 1859

Capt. Walter R. Ross d. June 27, 1850 aged 57

William Clarence Wilburn 1889-1846

Essie Phillips Wilburn wife Mar. 2, 1898-Aug. 21, 1942
* *(Hollis-Abernethy Averys)

Kate Fagen wife of Eugene Avery 1853-1934

Edward A. Fagen 1847-1930 Co. A. 62 Ala. Regt. (Southern Cross of Honor)

Marja J. George dau of Geo. & Lydia Dillard. Kings Mountain Co. Va. 1860

James Wilson Stephenson 1854-1928

D.G. Stephenson 1825-1867

McFaddins   Dobbins (Dabbins??)

Mary dau of James and Sara Frierson m. W.B. Mitchell

Mother: Matilda George d. June 4, 1871 92nd year

EATMAN CEMETERY

(** Back of Mary Julia Middleton Lewiston)

Irving and Judith (Taylor) Eatman first to come to Greene

(Graves in this cemetery but no tomb)**

Caroline dau. of John & Elizabeth Eatman Sept. 1893-Aug. 1840

Son of John & Elizabeth 1816?

Infant son of John & Elizabeth Eatman 18, Aug. 1850

EATMAN CEMETERY

Temperance Harrison wife of Wm. Harrison Mar. 25, 1787 Aug. 6, 1836

Jethro B. son of Wm. and Mary Eatman Feb. 14, 1835-Apr. 28, 1837

William Eatman d. May 23, 1837 aged about 35 yrs.

W.B. Eatman son of Redding and Sarah Eatman July 9, 1837-Mar. 27, 1838 age 8 mo. 18 da.

Inf. son of Thomas and Mary Eatman May 14, 1848-Jan 2, 1849

ELLIS CEMETERY

**Ellis in Clyde Jones yard: Lewiston, Ala. Greene Co.

Wm. Ellis b. Jan. 14, 1783 in Picken Co. Ala.
Wife Treacy Ellis Aug. 19, 1794-July 5, 1846
Son Cofield Aug. 18, 1833-Oct. 15, 1842

Ephraim T. Burton 1801-1860 **Ruth Scales grandfather

Nancy wife of Ephraim Burton 1815-1850

Rebecca Cooper d. 1849 aged 56

Mrs. Nancy Ellis 1823-1912

Elijah Ellis Sr. 1819-1875

J.N. Morrow 1860-1893

Margaret E wife of J.N. Morrow 1856-1890 **(see Hines)

Reeder Holly 1867-1941

Mary Roebuck 1871-1931

Mrs. H.A. Storey 1834-1878

Hattie Storey 1866-1895

Greshal Williams 1814-1894

Huldah his wife 1821-1894

James G. (**or C.) Hamilton 1850-1917

Mary F. Edwards wife of James G. Hamilton Mar. 3, 1847-May 6, 1914

Phoebe Hamilton 1876-1945

Rianna E. Williams 1869-1892

W.R. Thornton 1819-1885

Mary, his wife 1824-1897

Sam Snoddy Thornton 1846-1922

Clara Neal wife of S.S. Thornton 1852-1931

Thomas William Cobb 1844-1911

Medora Steele wife of Thomas Cobb 1851-1925
**Mrs. Herbert Gosa's parents. Daughter of Harriet Gordon.

J. Gideon Steele b. Oct. 4, 1832 d. June 26, 1859
**Perliahs father of Medora Steele b. 1859 (1) d. 1925

Joseph Cartee 1823-1908

Sara Caroline Cartee 1819-1884

Elijah Sellars 1820-1889

Nancy J. Sellars 1829-1913

A.C. Lewis 1849-1930

Malisa Lewis 1846-1932

W.M. Brantley Durrett 1874-1952

John W. Rhodes and Annie B. Rhodes
    1867-1939   1872-1946

Travis Taylor 1896-1924

Ida T. Sulzby Oct. 7, 1876-Sept. 3, 1895
**On her tomb:
    Dear Ida,
    Thou has left us now
    To mourn for thee below
    To a better home thou Spirit pure
    Was early called to go.
    Thy laughing eyes and pleasant smile
    Will greet us here no more,
    For thou art with the angels now
    Upon a brighter shore.
        From a loving husband

E.S. Thompson Nov. 6, 1836-June 20, 1900 or 1 **A Confed. Soldier
Southern Cross of Honor

Wife Sara A. Thompson June 22, 1846-Oct. 1, 1927

Willie Elbert Mize 1874-1952
Kate Mize 1850-1933
Wm. Samuel Mize 1892-1920

John T. Mize C. S. A. Southern Cross of Honor

Pressley R. Rhodes Co. G. 40 Ala. Inf. C. S. A.

Inf daughter W. E. and M. J. Rhodes

James Z. son of F. and L. E. Stephens 1881-1902

Wood Stephens Ala. Pvt. 166 Inf. 42 Div. Mar. 23, 1890-Mar. 8, 1944

Inf. dau. of J. & J. Nickerson

Sedan S. Eatman

Cornelia, Wife 1856-1920

EUTAW CEMETERY
Eutaw, Ala.

Wm. Howell Harry Ala. Pvt. U. S. Army WWI Dec. 23, 1889

Col. James S. Wallace's wife Eliza C. d. June 25, 1907 age 82

Percy W. Gordon 1882-1949

Capt. Jacob Wiyzer native of Penn. b. Jan 9, 1787 d. 57 years of age.
_____21, 1956

Wm T. Wiyzer 1820

James Roden b. Jan 10, 1777 - Nov. 9, 1854

Sara Roden Dau of James Dunlap b. Dec. 13, 1795-Aug. d. 1852

James Dunlap b. Abbeville dist S. C. Mar 25, 1803 d. Greene Co. Mar. 21, 1867

Mary E. Jones wife of Digges Payner Jan 19, 1848-Dec. 31, 1936 b. DeKalb, Miss

Digges Payner Lawrenceville, Va. Nov. 14, 1835 - Apr. 17, 1916

Anna wife of W. A. Gordon Feb. 28, 1861-June 22, 1919

W. A. Gordon Jan 29, 1858 - Sept. 1, 1935

Rev. Israel G. Smith b. Oct. 4, 1817-Feb. 16, 1893 (Mason)

John C. Smith Dec. 14, 1857 - Oct. 17, 1909

Jennie Perrin Smith Apr. 12, 1869 - Apr. 18, 1944

Victoria Hall & Foster C. Edwards in lot with Rev. Israel Smith. (**Foster Edwards Mrs. Gertrude Colson's grandfather)**

Fred A. Gordon

Inf. of R. C. and M. L. Collins Dec. 1888

Samuel Taylor b. Pendleton S. S. Mar. 1, 1777, Sept. 30, 1833

W. S. Taylor b. May 28, 1815-Sept. 16, 1836 age 21

Wm M. Pettigrew b. Sept. 21, 1843-May 29, 1871

Jane Edwards consort of Wm C. Edwards d. Dec. 31, 1851 age 46

Thos. J. Anderson b. Jan 14, 1830-Apr. 8, 1906
Martha D.   "   Dec. 13, 1837-Dec. 3, 1904

Olivia Almeda wife of T. J. Price Aug. 16, 1838 Feb. 17, 1905

An & May Shelton

Va. Brown Winn wife of Thos Winn 1863-1906

Annie Brown wife of Frank Inge Jan 2, 1912 age 40

Hiram Calvin Nov. 4, 1831

Ellen V. dau of J. C. & I Anderson Oct. 26, 1886-June 21, 1888

Harriet Dunlap Coleman 1851-1903

James C. Coleman 1842-1912 Confed. Vet.

Lightfoots

Geo. H. Dunlap June 30, 1807-Jan. 28, 1892

Louisa   "   wife Apr. 9, 1807-June 10, 1881

Geo. & Delida Smith Dumfries Va. dau Mary Va.

Alice dau. of A. M. & M. W. Pippen Mar. 16, 1864-July 24, 1904 **(A. M. is Littleberry's brother)**

Augusta May wife of H. G. Eatman 1862-1890

Charles Alva Pippen Mar 12, 1836-Feb. 24, 1873

Martha A. W. Pippen wife of A. M. Pippen Feb. 28, 1833-Mar. 9, 1873

Sallie F. wife of A. M. Pippen Sept. 1, 1838-Oct. 12, 1897

R. M. Pippen Dec. 21, 1828-June 8, 1901

John R. Taylor 1850-1904 **(owned Abrams place)**

Wife Mary Etta *(Barnes)** 1855-1918

Nannie Dew dau. J. R. & M E. Taylor

F. H. Munda 1837-1896

Mary C. Bray wife of Albert C. Hill 1858-1900

Caswell Bray 1808-1886

Mary E. Ward wife of Caswell Bray 1824-1901

Mattie Eloise Bray 1851-1914

Geo M. Hickman 1830-1888

Wm & Sara Scarbrough

Eliza Ashley Todd Lexington Ky. 1821-1896 wife of Thomas W. Taylor

Nancy Foster wife of James H. Foster b. Chester Dist. 1795 d. Greene Co. 1850

Harriet Brown Lightfoot dau of Dr. Philip Lewis & Isabella Drummond Lightfoot July 13, 1859-Jan 23, 1941

Woodliff Bevill native of Va. died 1837

Kate Jay Anderson 1899-1901

Thos. J. Anderson July 13, 1864-Nov. 17, 1899

Winter Roberts Anderson July 22, 1898-Nov. 9, 1901

Martha Davis Hall wife of W. P. Hall 1848-1891

Sara Stallworth dau. of John & Elizabeth Stallworth 1815-1869

Crawfords

Sara Emily wife of Robt. Leachman b. Wake Co. N. C. May 5, 1820 d. Eutaw Mar. 13, 1844 dau. of Esq. David G. Rencher

Louisa Rencher wife of Wm Huff Oct 7, 1827-June 30, 1851

Col. Joseph Pickens youngest son of Gen. Andrew Pickens Mar. 30, 1791-Feb. 3, 1853

Caroline J. wife of Joseph Pickens dau of John D. & Elizabeth Henderson Feb. 12, 1807-Junly 28, 1829

Robert Greer d. Apr. 4, 1845 in 34 yr.

Capt. Asa White b. Georgia Jan. 2, 1793 died Eutaw Jan. 13, 1861

Hugh L. White b. Eutaw Nov. 1, 1841-Dec. 13, 1875

Alexander H. Falconer b. Franklin Co. N. C. 1800-1855

(See Wm A. Bell born in Greene 1821)

Mary Ridgway wife of S. Ridgeway

Rebecca & Robert Bell

R. L. wife of F. B. Tarr Sept 29, 1836-Jan. 1, 1897

Frank B. Tarr Jan. 28, 1836-Dec. 23, 1927 Co. C 11 Ala. Inf CSA

Percy Gordon 1882-1949

Jeanie Elizabeth eldest dau. of James H. and Kate R. May. July 2, 1888- Nov. 10, 1908

James M. May June 24, 1893-May 23, 1921

EUTAW CONFEDERATE MONUMENT
Aquila Greer Co. A. 5th Ala. Bat. Archer's Brigade
A. P. Hill Div.
North Sumter Rifles

Burks
Parker.
Perrigin
Perrin
Powers
Wilson
Stewart
McAlpine
McIntosh
Mobley
Lay
Kennedy
Horn
Hutton
Beville
Bibb
Blair (Forkland)
Bragg
Brown
Cherry
Cartee
Foster
Gordon
Col. James A. Anderson
Lt. S. C. Brown 43rd Ala.
Capt. Nathan Carpenter
Capt. Geo. H. Cole
Capt. Thomas W. Coleman 40th Ala.
Anderson Crenshaw
Capt. Robert Crawford
Dr. Augustus Duncan
David R. Dunlap
R. Bass Dunlap
John M. Gulley
John W. McAlpine
Dr. John S. Meriwether
Willis & Fred Meriwether (**one Willis Meriwether Named Geo.
        Williamsons grandau. Lucy Arrington. dau of Dr. Joe Arrinton &
        Lucy Williamson)**
Capt. Geo. Perrin 2nd Ala. Cav.
Capt. Joseph a. Pickens
E. D. Pippen killed
Col John A. Winston 8th Ala.
Capt. John James Winston
James Ezra Wilson 5th Ala.
Anderson

(UDC BOOK IN LIBRARY)

Drucilla D. wife of Wm. W. Hale Oct. 29, 1816 d. June 7, 1844 (1st wife)**

Joel Winston Jones Dec. 3, 1853-Sept. 4, 1871

Margaret F. Malone June 2, 1865-Dec. 23, 1932

Wm. McCracken 1839-1906

Mollie S. Colvin 1870-1901

Hiram Colvin 1831-1887

Mary E. wife of Hiram Colvin 1827-1893

Va. Brown Winn wife of Thos. F. Winn 1863-1906

Anne Brown wife of Frank Inge 1912 age 40

Maggie J. wife of Eli Williams

T. F. Wm 1856-1894

Susan Elizabeth dau. of J. L. and Lydia Stewart Loften 1878-1928

Geo. H. Dunlap 1807-1892

wife Louisa 1807-1880

R. G. M. Selden 1843-1890

Dr. John S. Meriwether son of Judith Pollard Chiles and Dr. Willis Meriwether 1830-1879

V. C. Murphy Oct. 1, 1845-Oct. 13, 1932

Callie May dau. of A. W. & F. G. Gray 1893-1899

Fannie C. wife of A. W. Gray 1869-1894

Dr. Thompson W. Taylor 1818-1876

Walter Chiles

Mary Esther Gorden wife of Edward C. Campbell

DOUBLE TOMB

Coleman	Mary Cross
James Cobb	Feb. 20, 1880
June 30, 1875	July 4, 1947

A. W. Howard 1841-1909 wife Ruth J. Robertson 1855-1932

Mary E. dau. of S. O. and Annie G. Gordon. wife of Cephas R. (K? ?) Walker Jan. 18, 1830-Feb. 7, 1857

Annie G. Gordon Dec. 8, 1805-Aug. 1, 1873 40 years or more member of M. E. Church. Last words "God is Love"

S. O. Gordon Mar. 22, 1802-Oct. 2, 1874. 40 years member of M. E. Church.

Harry Talmin Herndon Nov. 8, 1826-Aug. 14, 1855

Emma S. Copp (Capp??) dau. of Harry Taulmin of Mobile b. Oct 22, 1806-May 9, 1922 Married (1) Thos. H. Herndon, (2) John H. Copp Dec. 1, 1846 died Oct. 27, 1862.

Simeon Chapman d. 1855 age 40

Joseph B. Edwards June 30, 1842-Apr. 21, 1909

Mary J. Edwards wife of Joseph W. Hall b. 1830 m. 1849 d. 1890

***(See Clevelands-- Delia Roden)**

John Milton Winston b. Mar. 16, 1808-Feb. 28, 1847

Mrs. Lucy N. wife of Col John M. Winston died Apr. 6, 1849 aged 39

Jane. B. wife of Geo Cleveland 1834-1880

Geo Cleveland aged 48

Thos. J. Anderson Jan 14, 1830-Apr. 8, 1906

J. G. McGregor dau of _____& Mary Ann McGregor b. Columbia S. C. Mar. 11, 1840 married Benjamin F. Gordon Dec. 22, 1864 d. Sept. 27, 1868.

Nettie Jane Beasley wife of Robert E. Smith Mar. 7, 1877-Mar. 10, 1920

Samuel J. Gordon youngest son of S. O. and Annie G. Gordon July 21, 1846-Aug. 6, 1863 "Sweet be thy long and soft repose, Young soldier true and brave, No rude alarm of cruel foes Disturbs thy quit repose".

Nathan K. Greenwood Oct. 29, 1844 July 1861

Harriet R. Anderson wife of Beverly Greenwood dau of Nathan and Margaret Anderson Abbeville Dist. S.C. Sept. 11, 1814-Sept. 24, 1851

Beverly Greenwood b. Ala. Oct. 20, 1811 d. Greene Sept. 24, 1852

Anderson Greenwood died in service of his country in Lynchburg, Va. Aug. 3, 1862 aged 24. (Houston)
"Houston thou art gone to rest,
"Houston thou art gone to rest,
Thy toils and cares are oer,
and sorrow, pain & suffering
shall never distress thee more

Alexander Boyd Sept. 8, 1834-Mar. 31, 1870 Murdered by KKK

A.N. Shelton Dec. 11, 1854-June 21, 1924

May I(J?) Shelton wife of A.N. Shelton Feb. 8, 1860-May 6, 1944

Edwin Covington Hardy Methodist Minister 1823-1886 b. Lunenburg Va.

Wm. R. Hamlett d. Apr. 20, 1854 in 53rd yr.

Harriet Ann dau W.R. and Sara M. Hamlett Aug. 15, 1832-Oct. 3, 1842

Wm. A. son W.R. & Sara Hamlett Jan. 27, 1844-Oct. 23, 1849

Willis C. Hamlett Aug. 21, 1849-Dec. 31, 1867

E.E. Hill wife of R.W. Hill d. Oct. 26, 1878 aged 67

Gabriel L. Hill son of Gabriel D. Hill May 1835-Jan. 1867

S.J. Hill dau G.L. & E.E. Hill May 20, 1839-July 8, 1857

Mary E. Hill dau Robert W. & Elizabeth E. Hill d. in 19th yr.

Robert W. Hill d. Aug. 25, 1863 in 52 yr.

Tellitha McLain dau H.R. & E.A. McLain Nov. 20, 1843-Feb. 4, 1857

Malinda Lakey wife Thos. B. Lakey dau Robert H. Aselia Patterson Feb. 19, 1835-Feb. 7, 1861

Lillian Allman wife of Samuel J. Carpenter Sept. 9, 1865-Aug.10, 1935

Samuel J. Carpenter husband of Lillian A. Carpenter June 17, 1862-Dec. 13, 1941

Martha Durham wife of J.M. Durham Nov. 14, 1825-Feb. 19, 1858

Margaret dau. Martha I(J?) and J.M. Durham June 29, 1850-Oct. 1, 1851

U.C. Palmer Feb. 28, 1827-Apr. 27, 1874

R.D. Palmer July 8, 1819-Mar. 2,1869

Va. Jarvis Webb 1878-1906

John Prince Carpenter Mar. 8,1860-Sept. 5, 1915

J.Frank Daly b Philadelphia Penn. Oct. 31, 1835 d. New Orleans La. July 2, 1873

Annie A. Dorsey wife of John Daly b. England 1817 d. Eutaw 1860

John Daly b. Ireland June 21, 1808 d. Eutaw July 20, 1873

Patrick Daly b.Banby Co. Cork Ireland d. June 1, 1850 in 39th yr. IHS CROSS

Katie Louise dau James S.&C. Cunningham d. Sept. 15, 1872 age 3

John Francis son of James & Catherine Cunningham b. Sept. 24, 1864-July 15, 1867

John Kelley d. Sept. 18, 1856 aged about 40

Joseph Molinelli native of town of Borsonasca in Kingdom of Sardinia d. 1847

Emerson Perry Rhodes June 16, 1861-Jan. 5, 1938

A.D. Hutton ____ 29, 1870

Robert Oliver Perrin Nov. 3, 1823-Oct. 8, 1878

Annie Theresa wife of Gustave Braune b. Dresden, Saxony d. Dec. 22, 1863 aged 26 yrs 2 da.

Gustave Braune b. Saxony Sept. 17, 1822-Sept 26, 1898

Honoria Theresa wife G. Braune b. Ireland d. Eutaw Nov. 16, 1873 in 34 yr.

Margaret Augustus Braune wife of John McKinley Feb. 5, 1870-May 6, 1921

S.W. Roberts Aug. 18, 1860-Oct. 18, 1916

Mamie Boyd Roberts Sept. 1, 1870-Dec 27, 1954

Rufus Earl Posey d. 26 Nov. 1844 in 17 yr.

Mrs. Mary Frances wife of Dr. M. B. Posey dau. of Col. John J. Winston died 18 June 1843 in 26th year.

John J. Winston d. apr. 5, 1850 age 65 son of Capt. Anthony Winston of Va. one of earliest settlers of state and commissioned officer of War of 1812. Attached to Col Coffee's Brigade.

Sara Gould Pierce inf dau. Wm. F. & Mary E. Pierced. Feb. 6, 1848-Aug. 1 yr. 7 mo.

Frances Va. Pierce eldest dau. Wm F. & Mary E. d. Oct. 1, 1847 aged 18 yrs 9 mo.

Francis Constantine son of Dr. F.L. and C.C. Constantine Jan. 9, 1842-Aug. 10, 1878

Fannie A. wife of Francis L. Constantine d. Sept. 22, 1878

FORKLAND EPISCOPAL CEMETERY

Ralph A. Parker Feb. 4, 1889-Dec. 15, 1953
Hollie Mae Parker 1897-

Julian Keith Legare Feb. 18, 1864-July 28, 1947 Capt. Medical Corps.
World War I. Ala.

Hulda J. Hahb wife of Wm. Legare b. Tripoli Africa Oct. 24, 1828-Aug.
18, 1901 at Forkland.

Wm. W. Legare Jan. 13, 1835-Oct. 11, 1890

Alfred Young Glover Jan. 10, 1835-Jan. 1, 1915 wife, Antoinette Malone
Feb. 4, 1835-Feb. 15, 1920

Nettie Glover wife of John W. Blocker b. May 24, 1861 m. Oct. 10, 1883
d. Aug. 23, 1884

Sara Va. Glover Mar. 19, 1865-Feb. 9, 1951

Cato D. Glover husband of Emma S. Glover June 10, 1863-June 7,
1927

Emma Dephine Seed Glover Aug. 17, 1866-Mar. 17, 1946

Williamson Glover Nov. 1, 1836-Sept. 3, 1900

Cornelia Bevill Glover **next to Williamson. died after 1876
**died between 1876-1886

Thomas L. Glover son of Williamson & Cornelia Glover July 16,
1876-Aug. 16, 1886

Mary Sophie second wife of Williamson A. Glover Sept, 19, 1827-July 7,
1886

Elise Carney Dec. 16, 1882-Mar. 3, 1885
Clinton Carney 1883-1885 children of J.W. & L.A. Carney

John W. Carney d. Dec. 17, 1910

Elizabeth McClinton (no date)

FORKLAND METHODIST CHURCHYARD

Beville, Thomas b. Jan. 1814 d. Mar. 8, 1869

Beville, Mary

Blair, James d. 1908-1956

Caldwell, John T. 1832-1882

Holcroft, Rebecca June 28, 1804-July 4, 1892

Holcroft, John W. 1838-1924

Holcroft, Nannie J. 1845-1928

Jeter, Litius

Jeter, C.H. 1853-1896

Lay, Mary Frances wife of Samuel D. Lay dau. of James and Nancy Lewis b. Orange Co. N.C. Oct. 21, 1837-Oct. 26, 1908

Lay, Annie Elizabeth b. Shuqualuk, Miss. Jan. 9, 1862, died Forkland Dec. 30, 1891.

Lay, Minnie wife of John Bates b. Greene Co. Ala Jan. 18, 1859-July 6, 1887

Lassiter, Harrison 1813-1886

Lewis, James Gaston

Lewis, Cornelia Ann b. 1837

**Nanie's sister Joe Dodson M. Joe Bates

GARDEN CEMETERY

Susannah Brumley Sumter Dist. S. C. Eight Children d. 1842 aged 68

Charles M. Fort B. Jefferson Co. Ga. 1803-1866

Matilda Fort Chatham Co. N. C.

Elizabeth Eleanor Fort dau. of C. M. and Matilda b. Jefferson Co. G. Ga. 1829-1840

Jane E. Sherrod dau. of Jane and Ranchel Bonner

Dr. William Lyles 1826-1859

Harriet C. wife of B. B. Beall died 1843

Henry Newell d. 1845 aged 28

Thomas Taylor b. Fairfield Dist. S. C. 1794-1850

John Bonner S. C. 1780-1854

Thomas H. Taylor son of Thomas and Frances Taylor 1830-1850

Meredith Taylor Rev. soldier 1764-Mar. 29, 1844

James B. Taylor 1821-1847

John J. Taylor 1849-1898

Elizabeth Sherrod wife of Sandall Sherrod d. 1843-aged 25

Jane Crim wife of Thomas Crim Sr. born Fairfield Dist. S. C. 1789-1837 M. E. Episcopal

Wm. Henry Marshall son of Wesley and Ann Marshall 1847-1848

Jane K. Stone wife of Stephen Stone 1811-1857

Stephen Stone 1801-1871

Alfred Jones Confederate soldier Co. F. 41 Ala. Inf.

Winifred Stapp dau. of C. M. & Matilda Fort b. Jefferson Co. Ga. Oct. 2, 1827-July 22, 1856 died in Pickens. A Baptist.

Mrs. Rhoda Gilbert 1795-1874

H. B. Chappell Jr. 1861-1905

Dr. W. R. Stancel Jefferson Co. Ga. 1790-1860

Jane Riddle wife of Rev. W. R. Stancell b. Chatham Co. N. C. June 20, 1802-Oct. 16, 1868

Mary C. Fort 1809-1879

Mrs. M. A. Ball b. Washington Co. Ga. 1823-1898

Charley S. Bradley 1887-1910 Erected by Wm. B. and Mary Lou Stancel Foster Father and Mother

Mary Lou dau. of Dr. J. P. Cravens b. 1841 m. W. B. Stancel 1861, d. Mar. 4, 1913

Martha, wife of D. Holly 1817-1870

Rosa Lee Dill wife of H. B. Chappell Jr.

Sidney son of J. B. and B. C. Newell 1858-1862

Perkins son of J. B. and B. C. Newell

Betty G. wife of J. B. Newell 1836-1872

William Calley d. 1862 aged 30

Margaret E. wife of J. C. Bonner dau. of Wm. and Sara Calley 1833-1853

Martha Alice Cally 1833-1886

W. P. Calley and wife

Bridget Turner wife of James Turner

GAY CEMETERY

(The location is uncertain. Mrs. Marshall said that there are Gays buried in Pleasant Ridge and in a provate cemetery in the country near West Greene)

Wallace Gay Mar. 12, 1858-1898

Willie J. Gay 1860-1890

Delphia Gay 1819-1891

Ben Gay 1816-1889

Fannie Adams Garth Jan. 30, 1883-May 8, 1928

Bessie Adams King Oct. 13, 1877-May 18, 1956

Thomas Daniel Sept. 22, 1865 aged 60

William Daniel d. Mar. 10, 1863-aged 22

Martha Scarbrough Jan. 11, 1815-Nov. 6, 1863

Pemiah Daniel Aug. 14, 1852-May 23, 1871

Arthur Daniel Dec. 1, 1850-Dec. 7, 1873

Sarah E. dau. J. & M. J. Daniel Apr. 11, 1875-July 24, 1875

Geo H. Daniel son of John & Peninah Daniel Aug. 4, 1857-Dec. 29, 1870

Marcus C. Daniel son of J. & P. D. Daniel Feb. 8, 1860-Feb. 12, 1880

Lula G. dau. of D. & B. Daniel Feb. 26, 1876-July 16, 1880

James Bradley Lockhart 1875-1954

James Edmundson native of Greene Co. N. C. Soldier War 1812 d. May 18, 1854 aged 76

James L. son of Joseph & Tabitha Rogers Dec. 27, 1840-Feb. 27, 1859

Wm son of Joseph & Tabitha Sept. 29, 1845-Nov. 6, 1867

Joseph Rogers Sept. 1, 1809-Dec. 30, 1872

Capt. A. Geiger d. Nov. 6, 1871 age 54-4-10

Capt. James T. Meek June 30, 1830-Sept. 1, 1866

Martha Eliza wife of Redmon Rogers b. Edgecomb Co. N. C. Mar. 17, 1819-d. Sumter Mar. 30, 1894 aged 75

Lucy A. dau. of Redmond & Jane Rogers Dec. 12, 1839-Nov. 21, 1857

Jane Caroline wife of Redmond Rogers Oct. 4, 1822-May 13, 1853

Elizabeth Consort of J. M. Weston June 29, 1808-1858

Wm M. Henry Geiger J. C. & C. B. Geiger

Belle Houston wife of Wm. Henry Geiger

Robert Weston soldier of the Revolution Aug. 29, 1763-July 1845

Mary wife of R. Weston June 20, 1769-Jan. 11, 1845

Joel F. Pearson Sept. 18, 1802-May 21, 1868

Joel Pearson Carpenter May 4, 1852-Aug. 16, 1878

Ann W. Pearson Apr. 25, 1807-Apr. 26, 1879

Lula B. dau. J. S. & Mattie Windham 1866-1882

J. W. Gentry Dec. 18, 1853-Sept. 22, 1906

James Windham Mar. 14, 1824-Dec. 27, 1872

Warren W. Crimm (or Grimm) Apr. 25, 1821 b. Kershaw Dist. S. C. came to Ala. 1837 d. May 31, 1851

J. J. Little

Mary Little

Sara wife of J. W. Little 1833-1908

Carrie Alexzena 1879-1888

John McCaw Meek Aug. 6, 1855-Dec. 6, 1920 Rosa Little Meek Sept. 4, 1862-Oct. 25, 1943 **Sara's Father and Mother

Annie Ling Little wife of John A. Hayley Mar. 16, 1871-Aug. 22, 1895

Sara A. wife of A. A. Rogers d. July 26, 1891

Va. Hannah Rogers wife of J. W. Lee 1851-1893

Geo. L. Ware Feb. 8, 1892-April 13, 1940

John A. Hunnicut Apr. 25, 1856-Aug. 3, 1922

Fannie Elizabeth Halsell wife of John A. Hunnicut b. July 7, 1860-Houlka, Miss. m Dec. 22, 1887 Panola, d. Nov. 24, 1887 Meridian Miss.

Wm. Halsell 1887-1943

Clara wife of W. M. Halsell 1887-1942

Geo. K. Coleman Sept. 1847-Mar. 14, 1890

Katie wife of W. G. Carroll Mar. 23, 1838-Aug. 12, 1867

Father, James H. Bell b. Edgecomb Co. N. C. Dec. 3, 1817-Oct. 17, 1887

Paul Fulton

Lizzie Bell wife of F. L. Starnes Sept. 30, 1842-July 27, 1876

Mary Bell Fulton wife of Paul Fulton

Patience Amanda Bell wife of James Bell

Sara dau. of John & Barbara Morgan Feb. 25, 1841-Apr. 2, 1885

Augustus George Grove Mar. 31, 1814-Oct. 31, 1886

Mary E. wife of Dr. A. G. Grove 1831-1906

Tempe wife of F. S. Baker 1858-1885

Sylvia Jane Clanton wife of Robert Clanton dau. of Blake & Mary Little Nov. 28, 1820-Aug. 22, 1846

Lucinda Clanton Oct. 23, 1815-Aug. 29, 1849

Martha Louisa Mar. 28, 1812-Sept. 2, 1843

Mary Elizabeth Jan. 13, 1811-July 21, 1814

Temperance Jan. 14, 1841-July 21, 1842 (Lucinda, Martha, Mary and Temperance daus. of Robert and Sylvia Clanton)

James J. son of S. E. & M. J. Nash Mar. 8, 1844-Jan. 30, 1890

Susan Lyon wife of Andrew Lyon b. Columbia Co. Ga. 1808 d. Pickens Co. Ala. Mar. 21, 1877

Julia Augusta Godfrey beloved wife 1882

Luella wife of R. W. Powell Oct. 10, 1841-July 25, 1873

Adell Grove wife of Jack Houston Dec. 31, 1877-July 1, 1953

John J. Houston Aug. 20, 1976-Apr. 10, 1907

R. L. son of J. J. & A. S. Houston June 26, 1874-Feb. 26, 1890

Almira S. Houston wife of J. J. Houston Oct. 29, 1841-Jan. 1, 1927

John J. Houston d. Jan. 27, 1879 age 41 yrs. 1 mo. 27 da.

Anna M. Houston Dec. 4, 1869-May 11, 1955

Dr. W. D. Boykin Edgecombe Co. N. C. Aug. 18, 1829 died July 27, 1867

Dr. Benjamin Boykin b. N. C. 1797 d. Aug. 14, 1857

Mrs. Martha A. Boykin b. N. C. Jan. 1, 1804-Jan. 8, 1865

Miss Mary L. Boykin B. N. C. Jan. 26, 1823-Dec. 24, 1842

Mary Gray wife of Dr. Edwin D. Boykin Mar. 19, 1837-Dec. 14, 1872

Dr. Edwin Boykin Jan. 8, 1834-Sept. 29, 1856

Mary G. Cromwell d. Feb. 18, 1875

Lucie P. wife of Dr. W. G. Little dau. of Dr. B. & N. A. Boykin Oct. 19, 1837-Sept. 1, 1869

Clemmon Darden b. N. C. July 22, 1804-Dec. 11, 1841

Elijah Crisell d. Nov. 10, 1850 aged 11

Washington Bell

Caroline wife of Rev. O. H. Shaver b. Warren Co. Ky. Feb. 13, 1820-Apr. 10, 1849

** M. Willie Gill m. Eugene Stanton 1882 F-12

Henry M. Bostick d. Feb. 6, 1904

E. A. wife of H. M. Bostick age 60

Garland Bostick Mar. 1862-age 63

Edwin C. Dancy 1815-1891

Ida Manley Baker

Hassie S. dau. of T. A. and D. Baker Aug. 15, 1892-June 17, 1893

Mary Hardie 2nd wife of S. S. Stanton dau. of J. and M. C. Gordon Nov. 28, 1835-Oct. 13, 1866

**Jefferson Gordon m Mary C. Pearson Jan. 16, 1833 in Greene

Mary Eugenia wife of S. S. Stanton d. Sept. 26, 1856 18 yrs. and 8 mo.

Henry G. Stanton whose remains lie in some unknown spot at Lafayette, Ga. He was killed in Battle June 21, 1864 in 19th year of age

H. L. Stanton May 16, 1863 in 16th year

Mrs. E. J. Stanton dau. of S. & S. Wilkinson d. Nov. 21, 1849 in 26th yr.

Ida M. dau. of S. E. and C. E. Nash Nov. 23, 1862 d. July 21, 1866

Caroline Fay wife of Stephen Nash Nov. 3, 1833-Dec. 18, 1890

George Erwin b. Feb. 4, 1835-Jan. 15, 1910

Fanny Iredell Erwin 1837-1926

Rebecca Jones Nelson 1848-1907

John Erwin son af Allen C. and Catherine Jones b. Greensboro Mar.
1861-Nov. 29, 1886

Catherine Erwin wife of Allen C. Jones died Apr. 7, 1869 age 44

Allen C. Jones 1811-1894 Col. 5th Ala. Regt. CSA

Briggs 1821 **(b. or d.)

Thirza M. Cherry wife of S. G. Briggs Mar. 16, 1818-Dec. 12, 1884

W. G. and M. E. Miller. S. P. Miller, W. O. Miller 1857-1910

Alice Reid wife of L. J. Lawson

Joseph Lawson Feb. 28, 1855 (** b. or d.)

Charles Lawson

Nannie Walton Lawson

Lewis Lawson d. Dec. 20, 1881 aged 66 b. 1815

Jane Garner Lawson d. Jan. 19, 1889 age 70 b. 1819

Miss Lizzie Ellis b. Sumter Co. Oct. 20, 1861 died in Greensboro Jan. 4,
1892

Dr. William D. Haywood Wake Co. N. C. Jan. 11

Lucien Douglas son of R. and M. Hopking Sept. 25, 1834-Dec. 4, 1897

Mary Pickens Carson wife of Robert Bruce Douglas 1841-1904

Thomas K. Carson Mecklenburg Co. N. C. Aug. 23, 1812-July 15, 1890

Adeline Whelan July 8, 1842

Wm Spencer Jack Jr. 1902-1904

Stollenwerck, Mother & Father

Annie Erwin Stollinwerck

Charles Whelan b. Wexford Co. Ireland Nov. 15, 1795-May 9, 1862

Helen Whelan Oct. 22,1893

Archer Hunt Christian Charles City, Va. (**Mrs. Nat Cameron was a Christian)

Sara Freeman Christian nee Pierce, New Kent, Va.

Martha Jane Stark d. July 6, 1818 aged 45 (1773)

Drake's (**Wm. Mann kin to Drakes)

Hattie May dau. of Robert W. and Harriet O. Drake Nov. 16, 1878-Oct. 27, 1879

Harriet Osborn wife of Robert W. Drake Sept. 1, 1858-Sept. 16, 1890

Robert W. Drake July 13, 1842-Vov. 24, 1908

Mary Ethel Drake Dec. 22, 1882-Jan. 29, 1935

Henry Boardman Aug. 29, 1817-June 10, 1873

Augustus Benners b. Nebern, N. C. Dec. 26, 1818 died Greensboro Aug. 7, 1885
Jane Benners dau. of A. and E. Hatch wife of Augustus Benners b. Newbern, N. C. July 7, 1826 d. Jefferson, Texas May 23, 1881

Richard B. Hatter

Eleanor Thomas

Willie Hurt Dugger wife of Bolling W. Dugger

James Head

Eleanor Bretney Bullick

Louis Bayol wife of Sylvannia Stollenwerch 1890-1906

Major James Heratio Wileys sons   Julius Honore, James Edward, wife Josephine Bayool.

Mary Hutchins d. May 1, 1849

Wm. Webb Moore son Sydenham Moore b. May 25, 1817 d. Aug. 20, 1862

Amanda M (W?) Moore wife of Col. Sydenham Moore d. May 24, 1869 aged 50 yrs. 6 mo. 10 da.

Lt. Alfred M. Moore late of the Confederate Army b. Nov. 21, 1841 killed in Battle of Chickamanga Sept. 19, 1863

Benjamin Dillard

Dr. J. D. K. Levert d. Oct. 17, 1860 aged 22, 6 mo. 22 da.

All on tall Henry Christian tomb.
   Niece Susan Brown DeYampert
   John Flemming
   Archer Hunt
   Ann Jordon
   Betty Wyatt
   Mary Warren

Confederate Monument at Greensboro 36 Ala. Regt.
   Col. J. D. Webb
   Dr. A. M. Moore
   James Brown
   T. M. Rhodes
   Geo. Nuttnig
   WM. Palmer
   WM. Stokes
   Co. 120 Ala. Regt.
   John P. Rice
   J. Garnet
   Ben Bates
   D. Stringfellow

Col. Sydenham Moore 11 Ala. Regt.

Alvin Rhodes died 1866 aged 30

Charles Clinton Seed July 3, 1862-Oct. 24, 1900

Mary Quitman dau. of C. C. and A. W. Seed

John C. Prreck Feb. 27, 1848 aged 31

Maria Williams 1824-1897

Willie Bell son of Rev. L. R. and V. P. Bell 1874-1888

Julia P. Fowler Feb. 24, 1854-Sept. 7, 1856

Rev. B. E. Cathron of Carrollton, Miss, 1866-1890

Joseph Chapman Edgefield Dist. S. C. Apr. 1, 1810 d. Sept. 22, 1872

Alonzo B. Chapman b. Dallas Co, Alla. "Among 1st Volunteers from Greene Co. ala. under col. Allen C. Jones 5th Ala. Regt. killed by a Minnie ball in Battle of Seven Pines 31st of May, 1862

Benners and Hatches b. Newbern N. C.

**Amelia Carnes m. Jemison Walker
  Posey and Thomas H. only 2 m. when James Sims died
Henry Carnels 1833
Posey 1830, Thos H. 1830 Eliz 1837

Harriet Ann Boyd Feb. 16, 1854-May 7, 1855

Mary E. Boyd Jan. 24, 1847-Sept. 16, 1850

Rev. L. M. Boyd (Mason) b. Newberry Dist. S. C. Dec. 11, 1810 d. Dec. 12, 1870 at Marion, Miss.

Sara E. Boyd wife of Rev. L. M. Boyd dau. of Col. James Snedecor and Sallie Orear Feb. 22, 1818-Aug. 26, 1859

John Campbell b. Jan. 18, 1815-Mar. 17, 1848 **One John Campbell married Martha Harvey.

Mary Campbell Jan. 6, 1823-Nov. 3, 1842

Amanda Carnes Jan. 7, 1826-July 1, 1841

Henry G. Carnes Dec. 31, 1837-May 1833

Josiah C. inf. son John J. and F. Collins Dunlap Jan. 6, 1865-Feb. 16, 1866.

Drucilla Eliza Collins wife of Josiah Collins and dau. of Posey and Elizabeth Gordon. Dec. 15, 1814-July 19, 1848 age 33 yrs. 7 mo. 4 da.

Penelope wife of Josiah Collins Nov. 20, 1814-Nov. 21, 1881

Orlando inf. son of J. & D.E. Collins Feb. 17, 1846-Sept. 7, 1846

Posey G. inf. son J. & D.E. Collins Dec. 21, 1837-Sept. 20, 1844

Georgia Pearson dau. of T.J. and C.W. Derryberry July 18, 1881-June 18, 1882

Rev. James George Snedecor Pres. Minister m. Emily Alston Estes
Name on halls at Stillman
Rebecca Savage m. Moses Estes 1827 A-63 Greene Co.
Elizabeth Lay m. Elisha Estes

Posey Gordon Sept. 25, 1775-Nov. 10, 1830 **Posey Gordon son of Capt. William Gordon of Revolution War.

Elizabeth S. Gordon wife of Posey Gordon Nov. 14, 1797-June 7, 1837-dau James Sims

Olive C. Gordon Nov. 16, 1829-Jan. 27, 1848

Thomas H. Gordon b. S.C. Feb. 21, 1804 died in Greene Apr. 3, 1830

Jesse Gordon Sr. Sept. 26, 1767-Aug. 21, 1853

Jefferson Gordon Jan. 30, 1808-Feb. 27, 1861 **Jefferson Gordon married Mary C. Pearson

Annie W. Tilman wife of Daniel W. Tilman dau. of Jefferson and Mary C. Gordon.

Annie Eliza Bordon wife of Thomas Jefferson Gordon Apr. 12, 1829-June 4, 1851

Gulnaire Adelkiza inf. dau of Thomas J. and Ann H. Gordon Nov. 12, 1840- Aug 24, 1851

Samuel W. Gordon Jan. 9, 1822-July 17, 1842

Lycurgus inf. son of Wm.P. and Susan O. Gordon Apr. 28, 1830-July 24, 1841

Adeline inf. dau. of Posey & Elizabeth S. Gordon

Prnold Jolly (father) July 24, 1807-Oct. 11, 1876

Judith W. Jolly (Mother) Feb. 17, 1818-Feb. 22, 1870

Aura G. Jolly, A. & Judy W. Jolly, Mar. 4, 1841-Feb. 6, 1861

Sally B. wife of Dr. M. A. Jolly d. July 22, 1892 aged 45

Son of Dr. M. A. and S. B. Jolly Mar. 15, 1972-Oct. 4, 1878

Inf. son of F. D. and K. M. Parham, former Kate Mssey

David B. Phillips native of Tenn. died in Greene Co. Mar. 1, 1973 aged 59 yrs. 10 mo.

George C. Pearson Dec. 24, 1809-Jan. 8, 1856

Eliza Ann (**Snedicor) Pearson wife of Geo. C. Pearson d. Sept. 14, 1836 aged 19 yrs 9 mo. 4 da.

Col. James Snedecor b. Va. Sept. 15, 1795-Aug. 9, 1842

Sallie S. Snedecor wife of Col. James S. Snedecor b. Va. June 6, 1795 d. Mt. Hegron July 3, 1862

Eleanor Snedecor child. (**No dates)

Anne Blake Snedecor dau. of F. P. and L. C. Snedecor d. Aug. 29, 1872-aged 6 yrs. 6 mo.

James died young

Wright W. Smith June 21, 1804-Nov. 2, 1850

Mary E. Smith inf. dau. of W. W. and S. S. Smith

Wm. R. T. Smith son of Wright W. and Sally S. Smith Jan. 17, 1831-Mar. 1, 1859

D. W. W. Smith Feb. 28, 1837-Dec. 31, 1861

J.F. ? Smith Dec. 13, 1826-Feb. 6, 1867

S.A. Smith dau. of J.F. and B.F. Smith Mar. 29, 1858-Nov. 3, 1859

Susan J. Smith wife of William Smith Sept. 20, 1832-Jan. 31, 1858 aged 25 yrs. 4 mo. 11 da.

S.C. Smith (**no date)
S.L. Smith **(no date)
S.C. Smith (**no date)
S.L. Smith **(no date)   small markers.--seem to be
S.J. Smith (**no date)   children--

Rebecca Frances Smith Dec. 3, 1834-Dec. 26, 1932

J.F. Smith Dec. 13, 1826-Feb. 6, 1867

John W. Smith d. Sept. 13, 1842 aged 51 yrs. 10 mo. 22 da.

Mary Ann Stevenson wife of H. Stevenson(**Humphrey) Nov. 20, 1811-Aug. 10, 1836 aged 19 yrs. 9 mo. 14 da.

William Smith d. Feb. 4, 1843 in 77th year

James H. Smith d. Jan. 4, 1834 aged 39

Elizabeth Smith d. Mar. 1, 1889

Jemerson Walker Mar. 19, 1815-Jan. 6, 1852

William Henry Walker son of Jemerson and Zillia Walker June 22, 1853-Sept. 19, 1854

William H. Wood Mar. 3, 1837-Dec. 29, 1872

**Jemison Walker m. Amelia Carnek C-1, 852
    (see if Zilla was Zilla Carnes)

HARRISON CEMETERY

Jethro Harrison b. Nash Co. N. C. Nov. 15. 1790-Dec. 14, 1843

Anna Harrison wife of Jethro Harrison b. Nash Co. N. C. d. May 16, 1832 aged about 38 years

Mary Harrison M. William Eatman 1828

** (Jesse Horton b. Jan. 7, 1773-August 2, 1850. 1850 Census Jessee Horton 79-b. 1771 Wife 74-b. 1776)

James W. Horton b. Dec. 5, 1841 died at Manassas, V. Sept. 21, 1861.

Marcia L. wife of William Horton d. Oct 5, 1852 aged 32 years 9 mo. 28 days. **(Miss Marcia's grandmother)**

Molsey King wife of Berry King b. July 4, 1808 d. June 21, 1881. **(Charley's grandmother)**

Berry King b. July 17, 1798 d. Nov. 12, 1851

Wm. R. son of J (ohn**) W. and N. *(Nancy Jane King)** J. Scarbrough. b. Dec. 15, 1850 d. May 6, 1852.

Jesse H. son of Henry and Maria Edwards.

Jesse Horton b. Jan. 7, 1773 d. Aug. 2, 1850

Jesse Habbord son of J. D. and M. Horton b. Sept. 22, 1843. d. Aug. 4, 1844 aged 10 mo. 13 ds.

Mary wife of J. D. Horton b. Nov. 4, 1814 d. Nov. 29, 1843 aged 29 yrs. 25 ds.

Inf. dau of J. D. and M Horton

Sarah R. dau of W. M. and Marcia Horton d. Sept. 22, 1850 aged 11 yrs. 9 mo. 24 da.

Mary Suber Horton dau of J. D. and Julia Horton, b. Sept. 27, 1856 d. Nov. 18, 1857 age 13 mo. 2 da. (21)??

Our Grandmother **(was a Quaker) Sara or Sallie wife of Jesse Horton d. Mar. 17, 1862 aged 85 yrs.

Julia wife of J. D. Horton b. Feb. 20, 1817 d. July 16, 1858

Lewis Dunkin son of J. D. and Julia Horton b. Apr. 12, 1840 d. June 17, 1858

(The ink is smeard from water)--Creek S. C. Cemetery
  **1. Leonard Strait d. Nov. ?, 1823 aged 52 b. 1771
    2. Sarah Strait d. June 30, 1833 aged 53 b. 1780
    3. George Strait d. Dec. 9, 1843 aged 79 b. 1764
    4. Margaret Strait d. Aug. 29, 1784 aged 48 b. 1736 **

"Our Father John D. Horton b. May 11, 1814 d. Oct. 17, 1882

Inf. dau. of G. A. and A. S. Horton b. & d. Feb. 11, 1901

Inf. dau. of J. A. and M. M. Horton Sept. 30, 1879
**115 tombs in all

**(Black David and White David were cousins. Black David because dark hair, complexion. White David very fair. White David Campbell officer in Colonial army m. Va.=Mary Hamilton.

John W. Whitfield Oct. 18, 1842-Jan 2, 1929

Mary E. Seale Whitfield Sept. 22, 1851 – 1947

R.J. Caldwell 1883 – 1905

Mable Stokes wife of C.E. Ryam 1892 – 1927

Alberta Hutt Stokes 1886 – 1942

John C. Stokes 1886 – 1942

John Rufus Whitfield 1876 – 1953

Cora D. Stokes 1880

Elise Louine dau of J.M.&Willie**(see Hinton) Richardson b. 1918 – d. 1923

S.H.C. wife of R.C. Fulton 1841 – 1897

R.C. Fulton 1835 – 1906

Dr. W.H. Owens 1842 – 1898

E.B.&C.F. Mackey

Georgia Singley 1854 – 1892

Selh Farley 1834 – 1891

wife of C.A. Peary 1859 – 1892

Narcilla wife of James A. Madison

Ella Lavendar wife of E.G. Rice

Jesse F. wife of J. D. Wilson b. Jan 5, 1878-Oct. 1911

Julia Tutwiler 1841 – 1916

Ben J. Travis 1843 – 1876

David Campbell Pvt. S.C. Troops Rev. war Jan 31, 1759 Apr. 15, 1846

Josephine H. Hutt wife of Rev. J.B. Pool June 8, 1851 – 1877

John Walter Wilson 1871–1947

Pennie F. Wilson 1905–1930 m. Ruby Evans.

A.P. Jones Nov. 24,1849–Dec. 3,1898

Pickney and Taniariah Jones

Robert m. son of Samuel and Mary Campbell b. Mar.1849–d.Nov.1849

Mary Irene dau J.P.& M.J. Rice 1860–1870

Elizabeth Stephens 1877–1908

J.W.and C.A.Holston d. 1887

Dr. William McCrory b. N.C. July 11,1804 d. Feb.31,1890

Foster Tucker 1889–1946

Sara wife of Alexander McKane Edgefield Dist. S.C.
Dec.8,1792–Nov.10,1852

R.R. Duram b. Ky.Nov.9,1824–Mar.29,1893

Wm. Clarence Wiburn 1889–1946 Wife: Essie Phillips Mar.2,1898–Aug
21,1942

Kate Fegan wife of Eugene Avery 1853–1934

Edward A.Fagan 1847–1930 Co A 62 Ala.Regt.Southern Cross of
Honor 1861–1865 **(see Hollis, Abernathy Averys)

Sara L. Baskin. wife of J. A. Baskin. Mar. 1, 1790
Jan. 15, 1859.

Sara L. Baskin. Dec. 15, 1825-Oct. 16, 1849.

Mary Baskin wife of E. Baskin d. Sept. 25, 1900

Fannie G. Birchett Sept. 28, 1857. . .?1865

Carrie Birchett. Jan. 1, 1855--Feb. 24, 1865

William Boyd son of Alex and Elizabeth Boyd.
July 24, 1800-Apr???

John Boyd (????) Wm. and Jane Boyd. Mar. 14, 1856
Sept. 8, 1857.

Edwin Bridges. Oct. 26, 1801--Mar. 22, 1887

Martha, wife of E. Bridges. Nov. 28, 1802-Feb. 22, 1866

William E. Bridges. May 7, 1827-July 15, 1872.

John N. Bridges. 1844-1866.

Angeline Bridges consort of E. Bridges.

Infant dau. of S. W. and Ann Botchillon 1897.

Willie Truman son of S. W. and Anne. 1888-1892.

J. C. Bonds. Mar. 17, 1842-Nov. 11, 1912.

Cornelia Bonds, Wife of Martin C. Bonds. Sept. 10, 1852-July 7, 1899.

Mary Ann Wife of J. C. Bonds. Dec. 25, 1839-Nov 24 (??)

Annie D. Brown Jan. 25, 1860-Mar. 27, 1950

James M. Brown Co. E. 20th Ala. Inf. CSA

Mary wife of John Brown Feb. 14, 1858-1896.

Candice wife of T. C. Brown Apr. 24, 1847-Jan. 19, 1904.

J. M. Brown Jr. Feb. 14, 1869-Feb. 11, 1910 Mason.

Peggy Jane dau. of John and Polly Brown 1827-1873

John Brown b. Virginia July 15, 1799-Feb. 14, 1892.

Joseph E. Johnston Brown Nov. 4, 1881-Nov. 16, 1946.

John Brown Jan. 16, 1829-Sept. 22, 1853.

Martha J. Chambers July 3, 1825-July 26, 1842.

William M. Colby Dec. 10, 1807-Aug. 14, 1840

Mary Donaldson d. Oct. 15, 1846 aged 59 (Baptist)

Ross V. Eatman son of G. I. and M. A. Eatman 1878-1900

Lillie Fisher (no date)

James Free only son of W. M. & Evy Free Apr. 13, 1835-Sept. 13, 1851. b. Fairfield Dist. S. C. died in Greene Co. Ala.

Wm. Free Feb. 2, 1798-Oct. 7, 1858

Thos. S. Free son of Simeon & Eliza Free May 3, 1842-July 10'62

James Free 1808-1862

Samuel Maxfield Gammill 1828-1838

Melissa Caroline " July 2, 1825-Sept. 7, 1843.

WM. Gammill 1788-1848

Infant dau. of W. P. and R. L Gordon **(Rachel Ladaska)

James G. Hughes b. Union Dist S. C. Nov. 21, 1811
June 29, 1858

Jacob Holland D. Oct. 1, 1852 aged 94
Sara Holland d. May 13, 1851 aged 87

**Caroline Brown wife of S. T. Brown buried at St. Stephens. Huge tomb lots of writing. Betty Pool says)

Col. Joseph Hughes d. Sept. 4, 1834 aged 75 b. 1759

Father J. V. Johnson**Major Samuel P. Otterson b. Apr. 1, 1754 d. Sept. 11, 1837 (1754-1837)
Mother M. E. Johnson

Oliver B. Johnson b & d 1816

Fannie L. Jordan July 3, 1857-17, 1867

Sara Kelley Jan. 9, 1853-Feb. 15, 1932

Nancy A. "wife of Hinton R. Kelley f. Aug. 21, 1814-Jan. 1, 1882

Hinton R. Kelley Nov. 1, 1811-Apr. 3, 1897

Robert W. B. Kennedy Oct. 14, 1794-Mar. 17, 1828 Called to be first pastor of Hebron Presbyterian Church.

**Robert W. Kennedy & Mrs. Charlotte (?)married Jan 19, 1830 died Mar.3,1869.

Mrs. Charlotte Simpson Jan.19,1830 d. Mar. 3, 1869(wife of Rev. Robert W.B. Kennedy)

Lela V. Lavendar dau L.A. and L.M. Lavendar Oct. 9, 1870–Feb. 8, 1897

Louis Floyd Lavendar son of L.A.& L.M. Lavendar 1879–1883

Willie S. Lavendar Sept. 29, 1887–Apr. 29, 1925

John H.   "   May 15, 1845–Apr. 13, 1908

O.A.   "   June 11, 1850–Oct. 13, 1891

Robert S.   "   1823-1849

Willie   "   no date

Lamar   "   1862–1924

W.P.   "   b. or d. May 27, 1884

James L.   "   1820–1900

Sara Ann Lavendar 1826–1887

W.M. son of A.F. and Mary Love 1833–1850

W.M.A. oldest son of John and Margaret Love Oct. 30 1880–(?? water marks on paper)

Charley son of S.J. & L.A. McCracken

WM.H. Miller 1862–1922

Linda Miller 1870–1894

WM. Moore only son of WM. and Kate G Miller. Mar. 29, 1883-July 4, 1887 **Katies bro.

James W. Miller 1837–1876

Robert Hindman Miller d. at Vicksburg May 24, 18?? (water marked)

Malinda H. wife of WM. Miller Mar. 15, 1815–Feb. 24 ?2

WM. Miller April 8, 1810– Dec. 19, 1885

Joseph Mayes Aug. 18, 1784–Nov. 25, 1843

Louise L. " Feb. 10, 1825–Jan. 14, 1847

James Ross son of W.M. & M.G. Meadows

Margaret Opella Meadows 1878—1888

Mrs. Rachel A. Mayes Feb.4, 1825—June 24, 1846

A.L. Morrow Apr. 11, 1834—Nov. 11, 1863

Catherine Morrow Aug. 5, 1818—Aug. 17, 1848

WM. McCracken Oct. 5, 1805—Oct. 22, 1855

Cyrus   "

Susan wife of John S. McCracken Aug. 18, 1851—July 24, 1867

Dr. WM. S. Mayes 1813—1843

Martha Patton Feb. 17, 1782—Apr. 18, 1856

Martha N. (Nancy) Parham wife of John P. Parham
1826—1854**(Martha Nancy Mays m. 1849. M. R. C.-1)

Elmira Jane Rhodes Sept. 16, 1839—Mar. 18, 1931

James Rhodes May 11, 1830—Mar. 29, 1902

Infant son of L. and H.G. Rogers Nov. 29,1844

Mary Alice wife of Dr. Virgil Snoddy Dec. 5, 1851—June 29, 1879

Dr. Sam Snoddy Aug 24, 1809—Oct. 29, 1894

Elizabeth dau. of Dr. Sam Snoddy July 21, 1830—July 30, 1893

W.C. Storey Co.B. 2nd Ala Inf. CSA(Southern Cross of Honor)

Melissa A. Storey wife of S.A.M. Snoddy Dec.30, 1842—July 29, 1888
Dr. Levert Snoddy 1867-1895

Dr. John Storey Sept. 29, 1779—Aug. 30, 1862

Jane G. wife of John Storey 1810—1890

James C. Storey Co. K. 34th Ala. Inf. CSA

Leo W. Storey Co. C 11th Ala. 2nd CSA

Mrs. Mary E. Summerville consort of G.W. Summerville Feb. 5,
1820—Oct. 5, 1846

WM. B. Stringfellow Jan.17, 1862—May 21, 1890

Enock & Mandy Stringfellow 1860–1884

Robert G. Storey Co. B. 42nd Ala. Inf. CSA

Hudson and Sarah Upchurch

John C. Vallentine July 22, 1780–Mar. 9, 1836

E.F. White Nov. 27, 1823–May11, 1854

Thos. W. White son of A. T. & M. J. White Apr. 23, 1835-Oct. 16, 1837

Andrew T. White consort of M.J. White Oct. 25,1802 Sept. 14,1856

John S. White Mar. 21,1792–May 15,1859.

Mattie J. Wood D.1875

James Woodall Apr. 21,1846–Aug. 17,1906

Candice A. " Jan. 19,1841–June 1,1915

Mary M. "1850–1915

Elizabeth J. " 1848–1929

Emeline C. " Oct. 1,1836–May 4,1854

John " Feb. 5,1800–Oct. 26,1882

Elizabeth wife of John Woodell d. July 3,1880 aged 68.

Dorcas Harris wife of H.M. Harris 1802–1867

Hugh M. " 1799–1855

David R. " 1832–1856

Catherine " 1835–1853

Ann S. Harris wife of Joseph H. Harris 1828-1855

Eliz. P. Harris 1822–1862

John S. " 1828–1862

Elizabeth A. Harris 1838–1862

Hugh M. Harris Co. E. 20th Regt. 1827–1863

Mrs. Mary A. Harris   1825 – 1866

Mrs. Mary E. Harris wife of James G. Harris 1835 – 1855 (James G. Harris 1st wife I guess)**

Geo. Harris d. 1830-1864

Harriet Louisa Harris d. June 8, 1876
** (My Grandmother buried at Herbon but no marker. Herbon Cumberland Pres. She married Daniel Love Cambell 1st Daniel Love Cambell was born in Glascow Scotland b. Sept. 28, 1816 d. Nov. 14 1866 Daniel Love Campbell and Hariet Louisa Strait (my grandmother m. Apr. 16, 1862)

Mary E. Cmapbell b. Mar. 6, 1863 (m. Stith Hardy)

WM. Booth   ”   b. Jan. 15, 1866 d. Feb. 11, 1866

Daniel Love Campbell buried at Sardis M. E. Church beside brother WM. Booth.
**
Daniel Love Campbell m. 1st. . . . .
      ”   ”   ”   m. 2nd Harriet Louisa Strait

Harriet Louisa Strait m. 1st Daniel Love Cambell
      ”   ”   ”   m. 2nd. James G. Harris Cousin Lula's
grandparents.

**Mrs. Gertrude Jemison of Moss, Miss. dau. of Horace Gore has Gore family history.

Robert J. Cox d. 1858 age 23 Tomb erected by his disconsolate wife who most deplored his loss

Bonnie Dorroh 1906-1933

Holmes, Martin 1861-1949

Wife Mary Brown Cook 1863-1937

Joseph B. Hines 1858-1923

Adah dau. of A. T. & M. A. Bush Apr. 10, 1872-Sept. 3, 1873

Mary Jane and Wm. Chalmers 1846-1894

James L. and Mora Ann Shotwell

Wm Spraggins b. Edgefield S. C. Dec. 21, 1793-Jan. 24, 1860

Lucy Ann wife of Wm. H. O'Neal Dec. 8, 1829-Nov. 18, 1852

James W. White Co. C 41 la. Inf. CSA

Wife Janie White

Sallie Nolan wife of Sampson Nolan d. 1852-age 21

Argm Findley wife of J. K. Finley 1852 age 40

Hardman H. Dunn

Mary E. Kemp 1883-1915

Mary A. wife of D. S. Curry d. 1871

Mrs. Mary Pulham Curry 1849-1886 dau. of J. M. and P. Ingram

Oscar Evans 1845-1870

Samuel T. Bradford Co. F 2nd Miss. Inf. Spanish American War

Mittie Bradford M. S. L. Youngblood

Mrs. Elizabeth W. wife of W. E. Warren Jan. 15, 1828-Mar. 2, 1865

Mary Goyne d. Aug. 9, 1858 age 26

Dr. Henry L. Williams 1829-1911

Mary S. Archibald wife of John R. Long b. July 7, 1857-d. Dec. 7, 1911

John R. Long Aug. 25, 1835-Aug. 18, 1898

Aylmer Car wife of W. C. Chapman 1873-1909

Geo. I. Ragsdale b. Halifax Co. Va. Nov. 19, 1797 d. Pickensville Aug. 19, 1835. Tomb erected by son Lewis A. Ragsdale

W. W. Brown 1839-1900

Wm. O. Ferguson Fayette Co. Key. Oct. 26, 1813 d. May 19, 1853

Bryant Ferguson Fayette Co. Ky. Jan. 3, 1803-Aug. 18, 1835

R. W. L. Glass 1838-1871

Wilkins & Moorehead Carson d. 1873

R. B. Bunnell July 5, 1835-Oct. 24, 1891

R. J. Robinson 1860-1892

Matilda C. Coy wife of Robert Stringfellow Aug. 31, 1841-June 6, 1927

Andrew W. Partain Co. H. 5 Ala. Inf. CSA

David W. Chalmers b. Scotland 1765-d. Pickensville 1841

Wife Jane Chalmers 1793-1835

Inf. dau. Apr. 1835-Oct. 1835

Gershom Kelly 1803-1853

Thomas Jefferson Boyd d. Nov. 17, 1850

Sara Emily dau. of Robt. and Mildred Johnston b. 1848

Eliza wife of N. Drake Apr. 13, 1808-Mar. 10, 1850

Elias Hill Bush July 8, 1891-Aug. 11, 1956

John P. McGee Jan 13, 1836-killed at Chickamanaga Battle Sept. 24, 1863-41st Ala.

Nancy E. McGee Oct. 20, 1838-Oct. 15, 1897

Katie Mae Cox & Wm. Walter Cox

Wm. R. Rodgers Co. K. 10 Ala. Inf. CSA

Jonnie Lenora dau. of T. J. & L. M. Foster 1881-1890

John Leroy Foster 1897-1927

Alfred B. Cox Co. H. 11 Ala. Inf. CSA

Mary Alice Walker wife of R. L. Moore Feb. 2, 1861-June 23, 1943

William Alexander Speed 1840-1890

Rev. Joseph W. Easley Presbyterian Minister b. Feb. 28, 1852-Mr. 20, 1885

John H. Frazier Oct. 25, 1855-Apr. 27, 1885
Wife Emma

Ernest son of A. W. and F. C. Gray b. July 25, 1881

Aaron Morris of Palestine Tenn. d. Oct. 31, 1857

Stephen Jones d. 1858

Martha Ellen wife of R. B. Bunnell May 21, 1838-Mar. 2, 1918

LYON CEMETERY NEAR LEWISTON

Lyon, Martha A. b. Aug. 1, 1829 d. Jan. 28, 1902

Lyon, Kate E. **(Strait) wife of L.L. Lyon b. June 5, 1852 d. Dec. 7, 1886

Henry L. Lyon b. Feb. 25, 1802 d. Aug. 6, 1878

Mary J. consort of Henry L. Lyon Aug. 1806-Mar. 1856

Mary F. Lyon July 5, 1831 d.

Wm. B. Lyon Mar. 25, 1847-June 10, 1852

Thomas H. Lyon Sept. 8, 1833-June 27, 1843

Richard L. Lyon Feb. 3, 1836-July 1, 1843

**Frank Lyon, Henry Lyon and Martha Boyd were the only three children that lived of parents, Lude L. Lyon and Kate E. Strait.

1. Frank Lyon never married
2. Henry Lyon m. Dollie Lucius
3. Mary Boyd married Frank Petit

Mary V. Goree July 1, 1858-June 21, 1904

Joseph Albert Goree Feb. 29, 1854-May 25, 1929

Missouri Jackson dau. of John R. & Eliz. Mullins

Wm. Paschal Shephard 1865-1930

Mary Moorehead Shephard 1877-1956

Daisy Dean Ferguson wife of E.L. Pogue

Annie Pearson Newell

James W. Brown Mar. 11, 1804-July 20, 1894

Harriet Brown wife Oct. 3, 1801-Feb. 27, 1892

Miss Betty Brown 1842-1912

James S. Goree 1883-1931

Lucy Grow Thaxton Aug. 1, 1886-Aug. 17, 1939

Henry Thaxton 1847-1936

Lydia Whittaker McCulley nee Thaxton

Rev. Richard Wilkins b. Va. 1776-1848

Nancy, his wife b. N.C. 1779-1859

Starling Garner 1827-1910
Wife Mary A.

MOBLY FAMILY CEMETERY

Mary A(E.) wife of C.C. Mobley b. Dec. 6, 1846 d. Jan. 18, 1877.

Columbus C. Mobley b. Oct. 13, 1833 died Sept. 23, 1900

Joel Grantham (**my grandfather) b. Dec. 17,1817
d. Apr.10,1887 "Meet me in the better land."

Elizabeth D.(**Dorcas, Mary Mobley said) (Campbell)
Grantham wife of Joel Grantham b. May 20, 1824 d. Aug.
24,1893.**(dau Alexander Campbell)

Lizzy dau of C.C. and Mary (Strait**) Mobley b. Sept. 21, 1873 d. Jan.
15, 1877.

Infant son of C.C. Mobley and Mary A. Mobley (**Mary A. Grantham,
Dad's sister) b. Nov. 4, 1868 d. Nov. 27, 1868.

R.E. Mobley Sr.(**Mason) Nov. 14,1829, July 24,1903

John Bird Mobley **(son of Rad E. Mobley Sr.) Jan. 8, 1879-Nov. 30,
1895
"A precious one from us is gone
A voice we love is stilled,
A place is vacent in our home
Which never can be filled".

D.*(Dewitt) C. Mobley Sept. 11,1853 – Feb.15,1929.
Gone but not forgotton

**(Wife Priscilla dau of John Newton Hutton buried in Philadelphia, Miss)
(The above statement is false. Priscilla was the sister to my great
grandfather, Allen Hutton. They were the children of Francis Marion
Hutton the youngest son of General Joseph Hutton and wife, Nancy
Agnes Calhoun Hutton. Other children: Edward, Aquilla, Francis M.
Jr., and Sarah Hellen. All from Philadelphia, Miss. Their mother was
Sarah McDonald, dau of Allen and Kizzah Whitsett McDonald.)
O.N.Wiese

Mary G. Morgan "Mother" 1846 – 1919

Thomas A. Morgan "Father 1834 – 1888

Marion T. Morgan b. Feb.1,1866 d. May 15,187?

**(Wiley Mobley was father of Mobley brothers below) McGowans, Mobleys, Colemans, D. Graffreeds — — Hills Colony from Bunker Hill S.C.

Wiley Mobley*(married Maggie Ingrum) died left big family *(See if wife Nancy Crockrell)
Dau *(Aunt Lula's sister) Euphemia married Chapman. She died & Mr. Chapman m. Miss ?Mary Ragsdale. Euphermia & Mr. Chapman had son who was a very good doctor.
Oscar Chapman of Monroe, La. Chapman married 3 times.

C.C. Mobley*(Christopher Columbus (Lum) m. Mary Grantham Dad's sister Mary died when son Charles (Charley Peak Sanders married 2nd Mrs. Elizabeth Carico (Aunt Lizzie)* Had Shelton Mobley was born. Other children Gus, Bob, Imogene and Lizzie. (Lum Mobley m. 2nd Aunt Lizzie Carico).

Rad *(Ellis) Mobley m. 1st Coleman, 2nd Langford. Wiley C, Irving & Eugene were Ra...rip sons Henry, John, & R.E. Jrs. sons.

(The above information was included in the cemetery notes. It is impossible to separate one from the other) Also information below.

Larkin Lafayette never married, killed in war

Constantine Mobley

Robert (Bob) Mobley

W. A. Mobley (Mike) lost leg in war. Never married.

Engaged to Aunt Kate Strait. Samuel Strait broke it up.

Greene B. (Berry) Mobley never married lawyer in Eutaw. Must be Greene Jr.

One Greene B. Mobley dau married Capt. Childs. wife m. Gainesville Cene.

Lum Mobley wrote his father Wiley Mobley des he saw his...ms brother C...shot down & killed in war.

Wiley, Irving, & Eugene of Bell Co. Texas were nephews of Isarah Mobley?????

Cora Grantham b. 1865 d. Oct. 22, 1951

*I saw Greene B. Mobley Jr. somewhere in record.**

MT HEBRON CITY CEMETERY

(Listed as the Christian Church Cemetery in GREEN COUNTY
ALABAMA RECORDS, 1960 by Marshall and Thomas)

These are additional graves not listed in the above book.

Parham, William Brownlee 1852-1919

Cameron, N.C. July 15, 1866-July 9, 1839

Christian, Sallie, wife of N.D. Cameron Jan. 19, 1845-Nov. 3, 1928

Cameron, D.C. 1883-1946

Nathaniel Allen, inf. son of Jimmie and Frankie Cameron
**Christians buried in old Gainesville Cemetery

NANCES AT HUFF HOME IN PICKENSVILLE

James Walter Nance Aug. 15, 1855-May 10, 1858

Sarah wife of W. T. Nance d. Oct. 4, 1855 age 29

Wm. H. son of W. T. and Sarah Nance

James L. Hutchins d. Apr. 6, 1872 age 78

Sara R. wife of James L. Hutchins Feb. 22, 1804-Oct. 27, 1887

Avarilla wife of W. T. Nance Mar. 26, 1828-Nov. 11, 1859

Henry M. Jackson M. D. d. July 21, 1853

Martha A. wife of J. A. Mooring Mar. 27, 1831-Dec. 4, 1867

John B. Scott Sept. 13, 1828-Aug. 4, 1856

Mary Jane and son Louis wife and son of Caleb Parker

Arthur Theophilus son of C. and R. A. Parker d. July 6, 1856 aged 1 yr. 11 mo.

T. Eaton d. Oct. 10, 1840 aged 58

H. F. Eaton d. May 2, 1859 aged 45

Alice M. Eaton wife of H. D. Long d. Oct. 24, 1880 aged 28 yrs.

Julia Jackson 2nd wife of H. D. Long d. Sept. 21, 1893 aged 55 yrs. 2 mo. 12 da.

Mary H. dau. of W. H. and Emma Childe d. Oct. 11, 1877 aged 19 yr. 8 mo. 16 da.

W. H. Childe b. Dec. 23, 1826-Oct. 25, 1907

Amanda M. Childe 2nd wife of Wm. H. Childe dau. of Greene B. Mobley Oct. 22, 1828-Aug. 17, 1909 aged 81

Henry D. Long b. Russell Co. Va. Oct. 6, 1837 d. Nov. 30, 1912 near Gainesville

A. W. McMahon Jan. 24, 1817-May 8, 1889

Mattie McMahon

Jocob R. Metcalf b. Kentucky Aug. 10, 1815 d. Jan. 19, 1864 wife Sophie E.

Henry Paash d. Dec. 9, 1860-age 36-6-28 (???)

Walter O'Neal d. Aug. 13, 1896 aged 26

Addie wife of J. H. O'Neal 1858-1902 **Mrs. Bragg kin to O'Neal

Harriet Harris Smith "Grandma" 1838-1925

Walter Elmer Crow Mar. 24, 1862-Nov. 20, 1937

Duren A. Parks Aug. 7, 1853-Feb. 3, 1870

Hannah Wright Anderson "Mother" July 23, 1860 Large Cross
???Emblem**

Joshua Lucy Turrentine b. Dec. 27, 1849 at Gadsden, Ala. d.
Gainesville Dec. 4, 1910

Ann Eliza wife of Reuben A. Meredith Jan. 19, 1820-Apr. 29, 1869

Reuben Anderson Meredith May 29, 1817 d. Aug. 29, 1878

Edward C. Sanders Jan. 7, 1825 d. Apr. 15, 1873

Reavis Atherton son of E. J. and F. F. Browne 1871-1872

Geo. W. Edwards June 19, 1817-June 5, 1901

Phoebe Edwards Dec. 13, 1813-June 13, 1875

James M. Knox 1831-1869

Inf. dau. of M. B. and J. M. King 1881

David Gladney b. S. C. 1815-d. 1868

John G. McCracken b. Spartanburg 1798 d. in Greene 1877

Jane McCracken Newberry Dist. 1828-1868

Annie McGiffert d. 1866-age 19 yrs.

Mary Blair 1838-1889

William McCracken 1840-1872

John Alley 1819-1883

Mrs. Mary McGiffert d. 1862 wife of James McGiffert

David McGiffert 1823-1900

Mary J. McGiffert wife of David 1828-1876

William A. White 1851-1899

Jennie White 1892-1893

Martha White 1821-1900

David White

Mattie Monee dau. of Mr. S. M. & P. M. White

Janie White wife of P. Vassetti born in Parsley Scotland 1832-1897

Pasquali Vasetti 1812-1886

Mrs. Mary Archibald 1798-1888

Robert Archibald son of Samuel and Mary Archibald 1796-1845

Martha Pervilla White dau. of David S. and Lydia McCracken White wife of Dr. G. W. Parham

Dr. F. T. Holly

Frances Thornton wife of W. P. Thornton 1825-1852

Carolina Knox dau. of Matthew and Jane Knox 1842-1846

Matthew Knox b. Pendleton S. C. 1797 died in Greene Co. Ala. 1854

Sara A. Mayo 1829-1868

Moses White d. (or b.) 1845 age 47

Dabney McGehee 1847-1901

Mary Patton Archibald **(dau. of Thomas Patton) Apr. 23, 1859-Dec. 21, 1945

William Pratt Archibald 1851-1932

Dr. Thomas W. Pierce

James D. Kimbrough 1831-1877

Mrs. M. E. wife of J. D. Kimbrough 1829-1912

Pattie K. wife of Dr. Thomas W. Pierce died 1895

Abner Alexander Archibald only son of Abner Alexander and Annie B. Archibald b. 1866 married Minnie Pierce Patton Oct. 20, 1898 died Mar. 6, 1899. "A good true Christian suddenly in prime of life taken from his Mother and sister, his wife and five stepsons."

John Shackelford Colvin 1833-1912

Thomas S. Colvin 1833-1912

Isabella wife of J. S. Colvin 1841-1919

Mary Anna wife of John Allen Colvin 1844-1887

Laura C. Turner **(or Tinney) 1875-1941

Willie Calvin Cochran

F. A. Lucius wife of P. J. Lucuis Sept. 28, 1838-Mar. 2, 1891

Thomas Wm. Pierce born Erie Ala. 1835

Emma W. wife of Dr. Thomas W. Pierce 1842-1894

Hannah Christina Goehner wife of James P. Sulzby b. Yollenbech Prussie 1835 d. Knoxville Ala. 1910

Philip P. Sulzby 1859-1906

James P. Sulzby May 8, 1826-Dec. 11, 1878

Clara J. Sulzby 1868-1920, wife of B. Barlow Wells

Wm. L. Neville 1862-1934

Eulela Neville 1869-1947

Thomas J. Patterson M. D., b 1880 d. 1949

Willie Bell **3 sided tomb. - sister and brother

First Tomb Wedgeworth 1824

Williamson Robert Wynn, son of Erasmus and Jane Wynn Dec. 27, 1804-Dec. 11, 1815

Jane Anderson ???? Thos. J. Anderson June 15, 1778-Apr. 22, 1859

James A. Anderson Nov. 17, 1816-June 1, 1857

Hannas**(lots of them)
Martha J. Hanna Oct. 23, 1835-Sept. 11, 1863

Andrew Hanna June 16, 1838-Sept. 9, 1863

Thomas Watkins Southern Cross of Honor

Bryant Watkins Jan. 1, 1822-Mar. 11, 1890

Josiah Watkins son of Bryant & Lucy Watkins

James P. Garland native of Va. Apr. 24. 1780-Oct. 8, 1854

Robert Hanna Nov. 10, 1796-June 14, 1842

R. C. Hanna b. York Dist. S. C. Nov. 10, 1796-June 14, 1842

Fultons & Brittons

John A. Wilson Oct. 8, 1796-Oct. 30, 1842

Lanbert children of W. and A. L. Lambert

Hester Ann wife of John F. Harris Sept. 9, 1882-July 18, 1946

Osmun Appling Wynn Nov. 9, 1804-Feb. 17, 1877

Mrs. Martha A. Sturdivant Nov. 16, 1834-Nov. 14, 1875

D. T. Webster Nov. 21, 1837-June 18, 1881
Wife Bettie Apr. 13, 1812-Nov. 4, 1867

Capt. Noah Hampton Gewin Wife Emerett Ferrell Gewin b. Feb. 14, 1848 Mary Ann Gewin 1st wife d. Feb. 5, 1903
**Noah H. Gewin m. Mary Ann Chapman 1865 C-1-390

Dr. Thomas J. Anderson b. Akron May 18, 1819 d. in Akron age 75

Romania Wilson wife of Dr. T. J. Anderson b. Washington D. C. d. Akron age 52

J. Wilson Anderson son of T. J. and R. W. Anderson d. age 30 (no date)

Albert Peebles 1796-1846

Oliver T. Cummings Sept. 10, 1852-Oct. 14, 1892

Lucy E. wife of Oliver T. Feb. 2, 1860-May 28, 1893

William son of J. A. & M. A. Colvin

Alonzo Collins

John Walter Colvin Sept. 21, 1895-Oct. 1, 1901

John Wedgworth Sept. 11, 1824 age 35. He was first person interred here after organization of this church

Esther Wedgworth Sept. 11, 1832

James Wedgworth b. Pennsylvania Oct. 31, 1771 d. Sept. 1843

James C. Logan 1773-1840

Claracy Long 1873-age 19

Sanders Kennedy b. 1839

Martha E. Underwood 1849-1857

James W. Underwood Mar. 30, 1850 **(born or died)

Dr. Middleton Wedgworth Sept. 8, 1828 d. Sept. 11, 1889 Body moved from Macon, Miss.

R. G. Hanna d. Apr. 31, 1883
"I am tired Brother. I'm going home to rest"

Near the Williams Cemetery joins Williams land (near West Greene) Erle Norwood's notes.)** written and copied Apr.13,1964.

Father. Andrew Norwood b. July 10,1803 d. July 28,1860

Mother. Mary A. Norwood b. Nov. 21, 1814 d. May 6, 1858 (** Former Mary Ann Cameron, aunt of Mr. Nat Cameron)

Charlot Norwood b. July 5,1839 d. July 17,1839

Josephine Norwood b. May 15,1845 d. Sept. 15,1849 Daughters of A and M.A.Norwood.

Emily Norwood b. June 29,1847 d. Dec.25,1847

Andrew Norwood b. Sept.26,1849 d. Oct.22,1869 Daughter and son of A. and M.A.Norwood.

(** Erle's parents: David S.Norwood July 2,1851 d. Mar.10,1939 Georgia V.Norwood Feb.12,1860-June 14,1914.)

OLD BETHANY CEMETERY

(near Vienna----near Benevola)

Mary A. Carpenter wife of Sidney C. Carpenter and dau of O. S. and Polly B. Harris. b. Nov. 6, 1835 d. Sept. 23, 1856 aged 20 yrs. 10 mo. 17 da.

Nancy K. Carpenter dau Churchwell and Malvina Carpenter d. Oct. 18, 1840 in 13th year.

Harriet dau Churchwell and Malvina Carpenter.

Churchwell Carpenter d. Dec. 7, 1850 in 49th year.

Jesse Cother husband of Elizabeth Cother (Cather??) Oct. 16, 1839 (b. or died)

Berry H. Gordon b. Oct. 18, 1827 d. Feb. 22, 1867

William Gordon Nov. 22, 1797 d. Apr. 7, 1864.

P.A. Gordon d. Nov.27, 1857 aged 28 yrs. 3 mo. 23 da.

Maria Gordon d. Nov. 2, 1856 in 53rd year.

Mary Ann Minerva Harris dau of S.W. and W.A. Harris d. Sept. 19, 1845 aged 5 years.

Elizabeth Harris wife of Sherrod Harris of N.C. d. May 3, 1846 in 88th year. Native of Virginia and lived many years in N.C. then came to Ala. in 1826.

Laban H. Harris d. June 3, 1847 aged 23 yr. 18 da.

Hudson Harris of N.C. b. Nov. 5, 1786 d. Apr. 27, 1846 aged 59 yrs. 5 mo. 22 da.

Polly Harris wife of Hudson Harris d. Oct. 23, 1843 aged 56.

Tilman M. Harris son of O.S. ..(Owen S. Harris, Nancy Lo????g's brother) and Polly B. b. Nov. 7, 1839 d. Aug. 21, 1855.

Inf. son O.S. and Polly B. Sept. 5, 1856.

Polly B. (Ricks) Harris wife of O.S. Harris and dau of Josiah and Sara Ricks b. Dec. 12, 1818 d. Sept. 11, 1856 aged 38 yr. 9 mo. 1 da. Devoted Mother and member of Baptist Church.

Martha wife of A.H. Hopkins b. Feb. 9, 1831 d. Mar. 18, 1854.

Samuel R. Marriott Wake So. N.C. b. Nov. 25, 1815 came to Ala, 1835 d. July 31, 1840

Susan L. wife of John M. Slaughter d. Mar. 23, 1844 aged 29 yrs. 5 mo. 17 da.

Celeslia Alice Inf. dau. of T. and N.M. String (feller??)

Mary Taylor wife of C.J. Taylor b. N.C. Oct. 11, 1806 d. Oct. 23, 1856.

Sara Winborn wife of William Winborn b. June 25, 1804 d. Apr. 9, 1856.

Mills Stephenson b. July 6, 1799-1856.

James McCrory d. Nov. 24, 1840 aged 82 yr. 6 mo. 9 da. Soldier of the Revolution. 2n Battles of Germantown, Brandywine and Guilford Court House. He was one of Washington's life guards at Valley Forge and served his country faithfully during the war.
"Peace be to the soldier's dust."

Jane wife of James M. McCrory died Jan. 1, 1840 aged 74.

Janne Mixon d. 1837 aged 65.

Catherine wife of Robert McCrory d. July 23, 1845 aged 37.

Alfred Keeler born County of New York d. Jan. 10, 1838 aged 24.

Ophelia Horton wife of Thomas C. Buntin Mar. 4, 1848- Apr. 8, 1901 "Mother"

Thomas C. Buntin July 27, 1840- Mar. 31, 1900? "Father"

J.W. Buntin "Southern Cross of Honor" b. Mar. 13, 1843- June 11, 1922.

Harriet Jane dau. of John W. and Sara A. Bridges b. Warren Co, Ga. May 1, 1822- Sept. 14, 1850.

Zealous Taylor Nash Co. N.C. Mar. 7, 1790- Feb. 11, 1851.

Elizabeth Taylor wife of Zealous Taylor Nash Co. N.C. b. Mar. 31, 1808- Nov. 4, 1848 devoted wife, friend, and Mother.

Margaret V. wife of Vincent Buntin Nov. 22, 1813- May 13, 1887.

Vincent Buntin May 26, 1807- Feb. 18, 1850?

William Buntin Nash Co. N.C. Sept. 21, 1801- Mar. 2, 1853.

(**Harriet Newell Finnell m. Burks.)**

Zacharys Newell son of John B. and Mary Newell July 1, 1849- Oct. 14, 1868.

William Weaver

C.W. Williams son of O, and Mary Williams May 10, 1833 – Aug. 10, 1853

Sally (**Harrison) 2nd wife of O.S. Harris b. Nov. 19, 1816 (**m. 1865)**

Sally Posey Jan. 15, 1869- Sept. 1877

Hugh Marion Inf. son of Minnie L. Trantham 1883

Inf. son of S.F. and Minnie Crooks 1890

Emery B. (**Emis dad) Peebles Apr. 6, 1860- Dec. 14, 1895.

Pearre Howard son of P (**Pearie) H. and G (**Guesner) P. Jones Sept. 28, 1910- June 6, 1912 (**Guesner Jones)

Wm. Peebles 1865 – 1915 (**Miss Annie's Husband)

W.B. Peebles Mar. 19, 1824 Aug. 31, 1884 Merchant of "Vienna for 40 years."

Mary Ella Apr. 11, 1862- Dec. 14, 1871

Inf. son d. Jan. 1, 1867

Inf. dau. d. Sept. 15, 1869 children of W.B. and E.J. Peebles Nov. 12, 1867- Feb. 22, 1904

Ella Vivian Mar. 9, 1896- Nov. 10, 1897

Bettie G. Darrow wife of W.B. Peebles Jan. 16, 1865- Jan. 22 1915 (**Miss Annie's Husband)**

Eliza J. wife of W.B. Peebles Oct. 22, 1837- Apr. 6, 1895 (I'm not sure about this date-- it may be 1875.)

Betty Cox wife of W.B. Peebles b. Lauderdale Co. Ala. Jan. 30, 1836 d. B'hann Ala. Oct. 23, 1893.

T.R. Pullis St. Louis

James Harper Fowler's Battery Lt. Artillery CSA. "Southern Cross of Honor"

Janie B. wife of J. Mushn or Muslin Mar. 19, 1838 July 6, 1896

Wm. W. Whitten d. 1890

Bettie dau. Wm. & Temperance Harrison

Elizabeth J. wife of W.B. Peebles daughter of O. (**Owen) S. and P (**Polly B.Ricks) B. Harris born near Bridgeville, Ala. Oct. 22, 1837 d. Apr.6, 1874.

Mills Stephenson husband of Elizabeth Stephenson b. 1786 d. Oct. 17, 1842.

OLD ERIE CEMETERY

*(Charles Parkel. Erle & I went July 21, at Erie.)**

Sidney Swoop first son of Henry S. and Catherine E. K. Mason b. Feb. 17, 1837 d. Sept 11, 1844 aged 7-6-27.

Margaret Ann Torbert dau. of James A. and Ann Torbert d. Nov. 1826

Eliza Caroline wife of Philander Lavergy May 23, 1816-June 29, 1836. aged 20 yrs. 1 mo.

Henry Lewis son of Francis L. and Clementine C. Constantine b. May 3, 1831-May 23, 1823

Rev. James Monett d. Mar. 23, 1834 age 52 yrs. 9mo. 23 days (1st Preacher to preach in Green Co. Was in 1818 Methodist preacher cultivated a crop near Troy in 1819 removed near to Erie

(The following is a copy of a letter that Mrs. Marshall included) O. N. Wiese.
12½ on it (stamped)Erie Dear Sir: 10 Sept. 1827 I read yours of June with note against William McDonald. Benjamin H. Mann To Mr. Isham Kimble, Jackson Ala. Clark Co.

Col. Young L. Rowston located in Selma 1870 b. 1827 Perry Co. Educated U of A. Hardy's History of Selma

ODD FELLOWS CEMETERY
(Gainesville, Sumpter Co. Ala.)

Martha Augustus Mitchell (our Mother) Apr. 19, 1844-Mar. 13, 1894

Daniel Mitchell (our Father) Apr. 7, 1829-Mar. 11, 1890

James Mitchell b. Abbeville Dist. S. C. 1787 d. Sumpter Co. Dec. 17, 1855 (Mason)

Jemina dau. of Jemina & James Mitchell

Susan D. wife of James Williamson Apr. 15, 1836-Dec. 18, 1855

Virginia B. Williamson d. Feb. 22, 1858

Louisa Ann wife of Dr. A. H. Smith Jan. 6, 1823-Nov. 4, 1852

Albert Henry son of A. H. and L. A. Smith Apr. 7, 1850-June 27, 1867

Isabella McTurk d. Sept. 17, 1862 aged 24

Joseph C. Avery Engmeer d. Mar. 22, 1862

Thomas W. Beavery Oct. 18, 1818-June 22, 1851

Col. R. G. McMahon d. May 8, 1880 aged 66 yrs, 10mo. 14 da.

Reavis B. Woodson July, 1824

Lucie C. wife of R. B. Woodson d. Sept. 8, 1898

Lucy Chew youngest dau. of Edward and Malvina Herndon d. Aug. 24, 1843 aged 7 yrs. 3 mo. 8 da.

John Minor inf. son of Dabney and Margaret

Christina Herndon Woodson wife of N. G. Garth Sr. Jan. 1, 1889-Aug. 6, 1918

Nimrod Garland Garth Sr. Mar. 8, 1880-Dec. 15, 1938

Nimrod Garland Garth Jr. Oct. 14, 1909-May 9, 1956

Dr. Robert F. Stuart Dec. 26, 1866 aged 50 yrs. 6 mo. 23 da.

Martha A. Stuart wife of Dr. R. F. Stuart 32 in 1850. Sept. 21 1821-Mar. 10, 1863 "A Christian wife and Mother"

Bettie aged 10 dau. of R. F. and M. A. (M. J.) Stuart

Mrs. Virena wife of Hiram C. Ragsdale Mar. 1812-Nov. 1891

John M. Soule Apr. 11, 1812

Nelson Dimick d. 1868 aged 34

Carrie Frazier dau. of Rev. C. A. Stillman b. Eutaw Dec. 27, 1852 d. Tuscaloosa June 4, 1880

Fanny R. Collins wife of Rev. C. A. Stillman b. July 14, 1838 d. Jan. 7, 1868

Fanny Collins dau. of Rev. C. A. Stillman & Fanny Collins b. Gainesville May 31, 1867 d. Tuscaloosa Nov. 13, 1872

Martha Hammond wife of Rev. C. A. Stillman b. Milledgeville, Ga. Oct. 15, 1816-Aug. 8, 1863 at Gainesville

Sallie Dudley Stillman d. Apr. 29, 1864 age 14

Mary Stillman b. Nov. 2, 1847 Eutaw d. Nov. 24, 1870

Robert Reavis or Beavis May 21, 1852-Sept. 25, 1855

John M. and Virginia Soule

Augustin H. Harris Nov. 20, 1808-Feb. 3, 1864

Lena Harris Williamson grandau. of A. H. Harris d. July 7, 1869

M. W. Harris wife of A. H. Harris Jan. 20, 1812-Jan. 16, 1852

Jere Chapman son of J. C. & M. A. Brown d. Sept. 20, 1865

Jane Powers 1888-1935

Jeff Davis Powers 1880-1955

Chiles, Betsy wife of Joel Limpscomb

Limpscomb, Joel b. Virginia Sept. 4, 1836 age 76 yrs. 9 da.

May, Albert J. Co. B. 7th Ala. Cav. CSA

May, Thaddeus Theodore Co. I, 20th Ala. Regt. Nov. 25, 1841-nov. 16, 1916

May, Francis Taylor Co. K. 63rd Ala. Inf. CSA Nov. 3, 1846-May 24, 1931

Melton, Mrs. Ann d. Nov. 28, 1848 aged 61 **b. ca 1787

Parr, Mary S.

Spivey, Geo. b. Franklin Co. N. C. Nov. 2, 1812-Oct. 15, 1855

OLD MITCHELL CEMETERY

(**Lots of Peebles in old Mitchell Cemetery near Johnny Berts Crafts at Benevola. Mrs. Colvin went with me. Jean Abston says Mitchell instead of Miller on highway past Homer Bambarges. Turn left at W.V. Colvins house (3 boxes)., about a mile to old schoolhouse and tombs in wood. The old Walker place back in there (Thad Gibson mentioned) July 26, 1960.)**

Found:

William Augustus son of John H. and Elvira H. Burns Sept. 27, 1851-July 29, 1852 (Elvira H. Maxwell)**

William Fortson b. Culpepper Co. Va. Feb. 28, 1774 and died at his residence on this spot Jan. 9, 1846 aged 71-10-12

OTTERSON CEMETERY ON COBB PLANTATION NEAR UNION

**John Johnson m. Sarah Gordon Dec. 20, 1827

Henry Walker b. Lunenburg Co. Va. May 20, 1774 d. in this Co. Oct. 4, 1856

Mrs. Mary Otterson Walker b. Feb. 7, 1786-Sept. 6, 1845

Martha A. Johnson June **(or Jan) 19, 1832-July 8, 1841

Mrs. Sarah Johnson Nov. 18, 1805-Aug. 13, 1837

Sophia Davis b. 1791 d. Oct. 16, 1830

Dr. Wm. (Will) Davis b. Dec. 24, 1791 d. Aug. 30, 1867

Sarah Davis July 7, 1817-July 28, 1867 in 51st yr.

Eliza Jane dau. Marshall and Mary Ren d. May 13, 1859

Inf. son of Marshall and Mary Ren b. Aug. 12, 1843 d. Aug. 17, 1843

Abel **(not readable) inf. son of Laton and Mary Upchurch July 12, 1837-May 14, 1839

Julia dau. of William & Mary U. Gosa b. Feb. 28, 1840 d. **so dim could not read.

Elizabeth inf. dau. of Laton and Mary T. Upchurch July 11, 1839-July 17, 1841

Joseph, son of Laton and Nancy **(Coleman) Upchurch Oct. 3, 1843-Dec. 9, 1845

James Laton, son of James & Nancy Upchurch Nov. 29, 1849-Nov. 24, 1852

PIPPEN CEMETERY ON HIWAY 14

(near Grubbs old store)

Mary E. Pippen b. Apr. 6, 1829-Sept. 29, 1856

Thomas L. Pippen Jan. 29, 1846-July 30, 1849

Willie C. Pippen son of G. and S. E. Pippen Oct. 25, 1862-Aug. 28, 1863

L. B. Pippen Nov. 11, 1819-Feb. 28, 1875

Amy Pippen wife of Eldred Pippen May 8, 1792-May 8, 1840

Eldred Pippen Mar. 20, 1790-July 25, 1858

Hixey Pippen wife of Eldred Pippen Mar. 1812 d. Jan. 23, 1864

Adison Pippen Sept. 13, 1832-Aug. 31, 1842

PLEASANT HILL CEMETERY

This cemetery record was published along with 13 other cemeteries in Mrs. Marshall's book, "Greene County Records". The complete list of these cemeteries are at the end of this record for those who wish to do further research. However, Mrs. Marshall had made various notes concerning Pleasant Hill Cemetery that should be included at this point.

O. N. Wiese.

**(Rina Sterlings grandparents were Hintons. Miss Rufie Rurnell was a Harris Her mother was Kate Lyon, sister of Lude Lyon. Married a Harris. Uncle Lude, Miss Rufie & Frank Lyon buried in Reform)

**(Miss Mable Corwin told me this: Fannie Williams m._____King. dau. of Wheaton Williams sister of Wheaton Williams m. Dr. Turnipseed.)

**(Miss Mables' grandparents: Dr. B. Turnipseed. 1919-1885)

One John Cockrell m. Nancy R. Lay

RICE CEMETARY ON HWY 14
near Caples between Clinton and Pleasant Ridge

Benjamin Marriott B. Wake Co. N.C. Jan. 25, 1824 d. Greene Co. Ala. June 25, 1873

Ida Rice Mariott dau. of Benjamin and Mary A. Marriott b. Jan 17, 1855 d. Jan. 2, 1872

Aley J. dau (B) * Benjamin and Mary A. Marriott b. Aug. 9, 1852, d. July 18, 1853

James W. son of (B)*Benjamin and Mary A. Marriot b. Nov. 3,1850 d. Oct. 8, 1854 age 4 years.

Aley A. wife of W.D. Rice b. Wake Co. N.C. Jan. 25,1824 d. Texas Nov. 11, 1852.

Hopkins, son of Aley A. and W. D. Rice b. Aug. 17, 1849 d. Oct. 28, 1849

Frank son of John P. and Annie F. Rice b. Oct 14, 1852 d. June 1, 1854.

Jane Rice dau. of Philander and Elizabeth Williams wife of Hopkins Rice b. Dec. 10, 17(6???)3 d. June 11 1838.

Neverson Rice son of Hopkins and Jane Rice b. June 30, 1831 d. Oct. 27, 1849.

Alexander C. Rice b. Mar. 4, 1835 d. June 20, 1862.

Martha wife of A. H. Hopkins Old Bethany b. Feb. 9. 1831 d. Mar. 18, 1854.

Samuel R. Marriatt in Old Bethany b. Wake Co., N. C.

(came to Ala 1835) Nov. 25, 1815. July 31, 1840

** Bolling Hendon Rice =m= Beulah Grantland of Nashville Tenn. son of John P. Rice.

SAWYERVILLE CEMETERY
(On left between Eutaw and Sawyerville)

Francis Taylor May Nov. 3, 1846-May 24, 1931 Co. K. 63rd Ala. Inf. CSA

Thaddeus Theodore May Co. I. 20th Ala. Regt. Nov. 25, 1841-Nov. 16, 1916

Albert J. May Co. B. 7th Ala. Cav. CSA

Geo. Spivey, Franklin Co. N. C. Nov. 2, 1812-Oct. 15, 1855

**1848 Tax list Greensboro Ann Melton by G. B. Spivey
**Wm. A. Melton
Mrs. Ann Melton d. Nov. 28, 1848 aged 61
**Apr. 20, 1760-d. Nov. 15, 1847

Betsey Chiles wife of Joel Lipscomb

**Land patent Joel Lipscomb heirs-m-Aug. 26, 1779
Joel Lipscomb (??writing not clear-Wiese) 1836 Aged 76 Rev. soldier
(See Gillispie) National Genealogical Registery. Will bears date Apr. 30
1834 Joel Lipscomb m. Mary Fleming.
J. Powel Lipscomb 1830 census Greene Co. (See Revolutionary
soldiers in Ala.) Book V
(The above notes were written in between the cemetery
information-Wiese)

Moody H. May Fr. 11 Ala. Regt. Volunteers known as Greene Co. Grays
on muster roll. No tomb**

T. T. May Thaddens Theodore Co. I 20th Ala. Regment on muster roll of
   "Planters Guards" A. P. May same as T. T. May Co. I 20th Ala. Regt.

   Joeph Miller at Garretts 1855

SHADY GROVE METHODIST CHURCH CEMETERY
Panola, Ala.

Betty Lee wife of W.G. Brockway Sept. 15, 1888-Apr. 15, 1941

Robert Gray Oliver 1873-1949

Clayte K. Oliver Aug. 18, 1892-Jan. 3, 1937

William S. Oliver Feb. 16, 1902-May 6, 1932

Sallie Connor wife of W.S. Oliver Mar. 25, 1867-July 5, 1947

Robert Perrin Oliver Sept. 28, 1844-Feb. 10, 1905

Annie Speight d. Oct. 17, 1895 aged 50 yrs. 6 mo. 19 da.

Two infants of J.T. and Mary L. Jenkins b. June 29, 1861

William Seth Oliver Sept. 29, 1866-Oct. 12, 1912

Sallie Connor dau. W.S. and S.C. Oliver 1899-1900

Llewellyn Goode Oliver Sept. 8, 1868-Dec. 26, 1949

Annie Connor wife of L.G. Oliver Feb. 27, 1869 d. Feb. 2, 1931

Wm. Goode Oliver son of L.and A. Oliver July 31, 1894-Aug. 20, 1898

Sophia Gray Rogers 1860-1943 **Walters Mother

James Pinchkney Rogers 1859-1936 **Father-in-law

Willie Little Bell (Mother) Dec. 17, 1867-Feb. 11, 1914

Seth S. Little Apr. 4, 1842-Nov. 29, 1879

Mary Elizabeth wife of Seth Little Aug. 30, 1843-Jan. 15, 1926

Paul Carr Jr. son of Dr. P.E. Carr 1892-1893

Julia T. wife of Dr. P.E. Carr Jan. 10, 1873-June 19, 1898

Ray Bacon son C & P F. Grove Oct. 2, 1881-July 23, 1897

Leonard inf. son Clarence and Peninah F. Grove Aug. 19, 1880-Sept. 3, 1880

Patience Turner b. Wayne Co. N.C. Nov. 18, 1779-Feb. 1, 1851 aged 70 yrs. 3 mo. 13 da. Tomb by her surviving children, Ben, Henry, and Elizabeth.

Noah Little Oct. 8, 1832-Aug. 2, 1899

Dau. of Robert and Pricilla Reid d. May 19, 1850 age 18 yr. 7 mo. 6 da.

Charles Henry son of Seith and Elizabeth Little May 7, 1854-May 31, 1855

Sophie L. Thigpen d. May 26, 1860-aged 27 **Mother

Edward Erle Taylor 1878-1935

Laura Taylor Peters 1876-1955

Wm. White Taylor 1875-1946

Ella May Taylor 1875-1955

Joe Creed EM 2C US Navy Foster son of Laura Taylor Peters lost at sea U.S.S. Houston Feb. 28, 1942

Samuel W. Barnes Mar. 3, 1832-Sept. 10, 1882 (Father)
Harriet Ann Barnes Feb. 9, 1842-Apr. 21, 1879 (Mother)
Son of S.W. and H.A. Barnes Dec. 14, 1860-Oct. 1, 1872

Inf. son of John W. and Annie M. Cook June 3, 1888
Inf. dau. of John W. and Annie M. Cook Feb. 12, 1887

Annie E. wife of C.M.A. Rogers Mar. 2, 1839-June 19, 1874

John R. Barnes Jan. 12, 1881 aged 71 (1810)

Nancy A. wife of J.R. Barnes Oct. 5, 1875 aged 55

L.T. Barnes May 10, 1844-Oct. 8, 1868

J.W. Barnes aged 32

Dr. Samuel Wm. Taylor Nov. 5, 1846-Oct. 13, 1908

Eliza Amason Taylor June 18, 1854-Mar. 4, 1880

Mrs. Martha D. White Feb. 24, 1824-Aug. 18, 1865

T.E. son of G. and M.E. Amason Sept. 23, 1849-Oct. 18, 1865

Miriam E. dau. Ben White b. Jan. 25, 1822 d.----

John Hare   no date

Martha H. Hare   no date

Rebecca Barnes   no date

Bennett Barnes   no date

Frank Grove son of H.A. and Mollie B. Morgan

James G. Barnes

Rebecca A. Barnes

Sallie W. Barnes

Margaret A. Allford

Mary E. Allford

J. Condre son of Wm. V. and O.C. Stanton July 6, 1873-Aug. 17, 1874

Wm. V. Stanton b. Edgecomb Co. N.C. Apr. 1, 1818-Sept. 1, 1837

Tempe wife of F.S. Baker May 27, 1858-Dec. 30, 1885

Frank S. son of F.S. and Tempe Baker d. Oct. 17, 1888 age 2 mo. (This could be an error in mother or son's death date. Wiese)

Capt. Benjamin Little Brockway 1874-1942

Chas. Augustus son of C.J. and C.I. Brockway 1883-1884

Wm. Little b. Edgecomb Co. N.C. Jan. 5, 1805-Sept. 22, 1873

Tempy wife of Wm. Little b. Greene Co. (**Ala. or N.C.) Oct. 11, 1808-Dec.5, 1872

Martha Blount wife of Robert Hibbler and dau. Edward G. & Martha E. Speight, June 21, 1846-Oct. 18, 1867

**Proved Apr. 27, 1863 : James F. Speight N.C. wife Mary Speight, son Seth Speight, dau. Martha B. Speight.

Edward Speight d. Feb. 15, 1863 aged 45 yrs. **will in Sumter Co. 2-275

Harriet S. dau. Seth & Nancy Little Sept. 11, 1835-Dec. 11, 1841

Nancy wife of Seth Little Oct. 12, 1812-Apr. 14, 1845

Margaret E. dau. of Seth & Nancy Little July 9, 1831-Aug. 6, 1846

Seth Little b. Edgecomb Co. N.C. Mar. 30, 1807-July 22, 1865

Laura J. Little dau: J.L. and M.A. Hibbler wife of W.G. Little Jr.
1838-1913

Wm. G. Little Jr. b. Edgecomb Co. N.C. Dec. 27, 1832-July 24, 1879

Maggie dau. W.G. Little Jr. and L.J. Litlle Aug. 14, 1871-June 5, 1879

Philip Edward son of J.E. and Ann Pearson Apr. 1,1836-Aug. 1,1925

Sallie E. Rogers wife of Wm.K. Weston Dec. 11, 1847-Jan. 14, 1925

Wm.K. Weston June 21, 1844-Nov. 18, 1875

Mimmie H. dau. Kelly H. and Mary G. Carpenter June 12, 1855-July 30,1857

E.S.Little Co.A. 36 Ala Regt. b. Aug. 12, 1837 wounded at Chickamanga Sept. 19, died at Atlanta Oct. 8, 1863

J.T. Jenkins 5 Ala. Regt. b. Jan. 7, 1834 killed at Union Mills Oct. 28, 1861

Mother   Lue Hill wife of A.J. Grove Apr. 15, 1849-April 1, 1917 **Kin to Miss Lue Hill McGowin--her aunt

Minnie windham wife of C.M. Quarles Dec. 25, 1862-May 8, 1902

Augustus J. Grove July 6, 1846-Nov. 10, 1920

Thomas S. Grove U.S.Navy May 3, 1890-Aug. 11, 1917

Ollie Atkins wife of N.B.Kittenberry 1897-1944

Howard Rogers son of G.F. and G.A.Neilson Nov. 7, 1883-June 16, 1894

Jesse Peebles Mabry Sept. 21, 1873-May 4, 1937

Jesse G. wife of J.P.Mabry Sept. 9, 1879-Jan. 10, 1907

Dr. Jesse Peebles Aug. 1, 1826-Jan. 29, 1900

Emmet A. Mabry Oct. 12, 1876-Nov. 30, 1892

Inf. son of Frank Archie and Bettie Neal Theroux 1923-1923

Waverly Peebles

James Irvin Windham 1870-1932

Bettie W. wife J.I.Windham Apr. 23, 1875-Sept. 17, 1905

David S. Simmons Feb. 27, 1833-May 27, 1917

James Neal son of T.P. and E.T. Neal Nov. 16, 1879-May 14, 1907

T.P.Neal Nov. 22, 1847-Apr. 21, 1909

Weston Moore Corp. 167 Inf. 84 Div. Nov. 17, 1918

Otis Young **Helen's brother

Susie Weston wife of T.O.Moore d. Feb. 28, 1908

Thomas Oliver Moore July 1856-Oct. 23, 1912

G.L.Weston wife A.G.Weston June 4, 1839-Mar. 13, 1906

Thomas D. (O) Moore, 92 Field Arty. 4 Div. Oct. 25, 1922

Maude Marine wife of B.W.Marine 1883-1923

Susan Weston Moore Aug. 27, 1920-Nov. 8, 1924

Essie Mae Hales June 26, 1906-July 8, 1932

Wm. L. Knight Feb. 11, 1926-Jan. 18, 1898

Alexander L. Rhoden Apr. 13, 1880-May 18, 1925 Devoted husband and father

Rhonda E. dau. L.B. and Malissa Cole July 1855-Apr. 24, 1896

Geo. Thomas Abrams Sept. 9, 1850-Jan. 17, 1918

W.F. Taylor Confederate Soldier d. July, 1882-aged----

Becker, Sara May 15, 1844-Feb. 19, 1915

Cockrell, John William 1863-1945

Friday, W. H. 1820-1899 **Lots of Fridays

Jones, Lula wife of Adam Jones d. Feb. 1, 1909

Jones Alford E. Nov. 9, 1827-June 1, 1815

Jennings, John Benjamin 1861-1935

Kilpatrick, Joseph 1830-1922

Mills, Bertha Thaxton 1893-1946

Moore, John Wilson Co. D. 26th Ala. Inf. CSA

Newell, Bedford Apr. 27, 1895-Aug. 20, 1917

Prude, William Dec. 27, 1812-May 3, 1877

Prude, Z. K. 1818-1885

Stewart, William C. 1837-1888

Stewart , Bettie wife of Wm. C. 1837-1899

Stewart, Rev. Joseph G. died Dec. 1869

Stewart, Mrs. Selina wife of Rev. J. G. Stewart

Thaxton, Wm. Dec. 25, 1810-Mar. 11, 1896

Thaxton, Sara J. wife of Wm. July 19, 1825-Mar. 5, 1892

Thaxton, Charles Madison Dec. 24, 1846-Jan. 17, 1930

Thaxton, Nancy Jane Mar. 8, 1868-Feb. 23, 1940

Thomas, Martha A. & Trust dau. of Wm. & Ellen Prude

Elizabeth Steele relict Abner A. Steele buried here July 2, 1842 aged 74.

Abner A. Steele Nov. 4, 1768 buried here July 2, 1842 aged74.

Jane G. Steele Apr. 13,1798-May 24,1869

Harriet C. 2nd wife of W.M.Hale aged 30 ys 6mo.died at residence of husband in Sumter on June 26, 1859. Laid to rest beside her 1st husband E. B. G. Steele.

Ezekiel B.G. Steele d. Aug. 5, 1855 aged 29 yrs. 3 mo. 29 da.

Medora Steele dau E.B.G.&H.C.Steele aged 21 months 13 da.

Joseph L. Steele b. Nov. 6, 1819-Oct.2, 1838.

Alexander Steele Jan.8, 1795- Apr. 5,1828.

E.R.Steele b. Dec.25,1798 June 26,1878.

Tenah Steele buried here Sept. 30, 1859 aged 58

J. Gideon Steele Oct.4,1832 June 26,1859

Linda Steele wife of J.D.Steele June 20,1838-Sept.17,1875.

Elihu Hatter Steele Aug. 7,1873-June 30,1886.

S.P.Steele 1829-1915

Abner A. Steele b. Oct 15,1809&buried here Apr.29,1841.age 32.

Mary E. Steele consort of Abner A. Steele b. Jan.22,1814 Jan.29,1841.

UNNAMED CEMETERY

(Located in wooded area on road between Homer Bambarger's store and Bush Creek in Greene Co.)

Sally N. (W??) Richardson dau. of Thomas Coleman b. Lunenburg Co. Va. d. Oct. 10, 1845 aged 39 yrs. 11 mo. 7 da.

Grady R. Hicks b. May 7, 1832-July 1, 1842

James Franklin son of John & A. J. Upchurch May 7, 1844-Nov. 8, 1852

Nancy D. dau. of J. and A. J. Upchurch Mar. 29, 1859-Sept. 22, 1868

John Upchurch d. June 25, 1871 aged 57 yrs. 2 mo. 3 da.

Newton Jasper inf son of Elizabeth & Elijah Fortson Aug. 21, 1842-Dec. 1, 1843

**Elijah Fortson m. Elizabeth Richardson dau. of Wm. Richardson in Dec. 19, 1842 Wm. Richardson Will C-29 June 12, 1843

**James M. Kennedy m. Nancy Wilder, I think. Green Wilders widow dau. of Wm. Richardson

**Francis Marion and Wm. Joseph were brothers. C. M. was Wm. Joseph's son. (These names were in reference to the Hutton brothers, sons of Joseph Hutton and Nancy (Agnes) Calhoun who are buried in the old Bigbee cemetery. . .Wiese.)

UPPER PICKENSVILLE CEMETERY

Henry James Lafayette son of Dr. H. W. and Georgia Brooks Doss

James M. Weaver Feb. 8, 1816-Mar. 22, 1891
Elizabeth Weaver wife of James Sept. 18, 1829-Dec. 13, 1891
**Mrs. Weaver dau. of Rev. Ellis Gore of McShan

Thomas Hopkins son of H. L. and V. P. Williams d. 1863

Son of J. M. and M. O. Foster **(next to E. R. & E. A. Dunlap) d. 1871

Sallie B. Hughes wife of John E. Wilkins dau. of Andrew B. Hughes and
Sara G. Long 1864-1941. Aunt of Sam, Mary & Sara White

John E. Wilkins 1849-1913

Alonzo Clay son of Wm. and Mary Permela Lang 1844-1872

Dr. A. M. Wilkirs d. Mar. 15, 1878

Buffingtons, Clards, Peterson, Eddins, Moorehead, Yagles, Langs

Cornelia wife of W. H. Horton Sept. 3, 1843-May 13, 1911

Wm. H. Horton Jan. 25, 1828-Oct. 22, 1895

Alice Easton 1856-1892

Albert J. Peterson Sept. 7, 1833-Aug. 26, 1895

Mrs. Wincy Azalee Peterson 1833-1910

Albert T. Henley 7 Ala. Cav. CSA

Sara his wife 1822-1888

T. H. Wilbourn 1861-1899

Arthur H. Carpenter 1868-1899

John J. Lee b. Union Dist. S. C. Apr. 5, 1814-June 30, 1892

Dr. R. R. Wyatt b. May 8, 1857-His wife Lyda Doss b. Aug. 2, 1877 d.
Apr. 26, 1926

Melissa Lee dau. of John J. & Nancy Lee wife of J. J. Ball

Wife of W. G. Gunter Aug. 20, 1869-Sept. 18, 1895

Willie Collins 1862-1891

Rev. Sardine Hildreth 1832-1892

Phoebe Hopping 1811-1893

Daniel Hopping 1818-1893

John Burglas Sr. b. Kershaw Dist. S.C. Oct. 14, 1793-Sept. 5, 1849

Geo. R. Thompson son of Joshua R. and Nancy M. Thompson Mar. 25, 1850-Sept. 25, 1850

M.E. Thomas dau. of J.A. and T.J. Thomas Oct. 30, 1843-June 13, 1845

J.B. Thomas son of J.A. and T.J. Thomas Nov. 22, 1841-July 5, 1842

Juli F. wife of W.W. Crimm dau. of Geo. M. and Elizabeth Trantham June 11, 1827-July 29, 1845. (**Large tomb)

Miriam wife of J.P. Lee dau. of G.M. and Elizabeth Trantham May 29, 1831-Sept. 1, 1849

G.M. Trantham May 3, 1793-July 19, 1837

Mrs. Elizabeth Trantham (**Could not read)

Joshua R. Thompson Apr. 12, 1825-May 7, 1850

Wm. Geo. son of James H. and E.J. Trantham May 9, 1850-Dec. 9, 1850

Infant son of James H. and M.E. Trantham 1854

Pleasant Hill d. Jan. 6, 1912 aged 80 (**born 1832)

Carpenter, John James b. Apr. 17, 1834 d. Jan. 14, 1857 consort of M. A. Carpenter. **Mary Addie Matilda Strait. Aunt Ad married 2nd to Geo. R. Neil. Neal Ernest Neil's father

Carpenter, Simeon b. May 22, 1800 d. Aug. 5, 1860. Consort of M. M. Carpenter

Carpenter, Mary M. wife of Simeon Carpenter Oct. 2, 1808-Aug. 20 1881

Carpenter, Mary A. b. Apr. 20, 1860-Sept. 14, 1866

Carpenter, S. T. b. July 1, 1830-May 12, 1862 consort of M. M. A Carpenter **former Mary M. A. Johnson m. 1855 C-1-155

Carpenter, John J. b. Oct. 6, 1857-May 4, 1859 son of S. T. and M. M. A. Carpenter.

Dan born Oct. 1, 1845 **no name

Carpenter, Alonzo Jefferson, son of Simeon & Mary M. Carpenter b. Jan. 21, 1842-Mar. 27, 1844

Cherry, Sara Sept. 25, 1788-Aug. 20, 1857 consort of Samuel T. Cherry

Cherry, Samuel T. b. July 23, 1779-Sept. 20 1843 **Sara's husband

Collier, M. C. wife of G. W. Collier Feb. 12, 1811-Nov. 17, 1882 **Aunt Lizzie Mobley was a Collier

Clay, James E. June 23, 1816-May 25, 1899 **first Mrs. Mayes was a Clay

Chapman, Mary B. Sept. 28, 1838-Dec. 3, 1911 wife of John R. Chapman

Cottles, Wm. O. Ala. PVT. 323 Inf. 91 Div. Oct. 14, 1918

Foster, Mary Aug. 30, 1827-Nov. 17, 1869

Foster, Wm. H. Foster Sept. 12, 1808-Mar. 16, 1872

Foster, Epayeth Dec. 15, 1802-Mar. 21, 1847 **wife of William H. Foster

Foster, Elizabeth May 23, 1830-June 25, 1836 **dau. of Wm. H. and Epayeth

Foster, Rachel Savilla May 17, 1841-Nov. 28, 1856 dau. of Wm. H. and Epayeth Foster

Foster, Stephen Weir Aug. 1, 1839-Apr. 5, 1857

Foster, Mrs. O. L. July 12, 1845-Jan. 22, 1872

Hardy, Mary E. Nov. 6, 1862-June 3, 1889 **wife of E. E. Hardy

Johnson, John C. Jan. 18, 1802-Jan. 11, 1856

Leavell, Mary Elizabeth Apr. 2, 1851-Aug. 15, 1887 **wife of J. W. Leavell. Might be Mary E. Hopkins

Lanford, Eliz. Bird Sept. 20, 1813-Nov. 1883 wife of Henry Lanford

Lanford, Henry Dec. 8, 1810-Feb. 2, 1883

Mabry, A. G. July 26, 1838-Apr. 29, 1908

Rogers, Annie E. Oct. 28, 1867-Aug. 10, 1870 dau. T. H. & M. A. A. Rogers

Rogers, Mary M.M.A. Dec. 14, 1855-Sept. 6, 1867**m. Willie C. Carpenter

Rea, Louisa C. Mar. 20, 1829-Nov. 7, 1855 **wife of John L. Rea.

Rea, Louisa A. Sept. 28, 1854-Oct. 20, 1866

Robinson, Eliz. H. d. Sept. 18, 1852

Singleton, Richardson Nov. 8, 1833-Aug. 4, 1863, "A brave spirit lies buried here who died a glorious death in his country's cause"**m. Amanda Hales Sept. 17, 1857 D-1-215.

Ragsdale, Wesley Mar. 2, 1844-Feb. 14, 1909 (Southern Cross of Honor) 1861-65

Sims, Lasey, consort of Capt. James Sims dau. of Michael and Elizabeth Wallis. Native of Laurence Dist. S.S.

Tutt, Sara Oct. 7, 1834-Aug. 9, 1891 dau. Simeon & Mary M. Carpenter.

Turner, Mary aged about 82

Taylor, Walter G. July 11, 1895-Mar. 22, 1918 (Died in Military Service Camp Wheeler Macon, Ga.)

Taylor, Ullman Feb. 14, 1890-Mar. 2, 1948 (World War I Vet)

Taylor, James Oscar Jan. 9, 1883-Dec. 3, 1934 Pennsylvania Boiler Maker, U.S. Navy

Asa White son of W.B. and C.C. (or G.G.) White b. Mar. 13, 1877 d. Oct. 5, 1883

**#32, One James Sims was Posey Gordon's wife's father. Elizabeth Posey's wife was guardian of her minor children (all) in grandfather's estate.

BARKSDALE-CANNON CEMETERY
NEAR SCOOBA ON LEFT SIDE OF ROAD
(Scooba, Miss.)

Nathaniel Barksdale son of John and Ann P. Barksdale native of Ala. b. Aug. 17, 1819-Feb. 22, 1949

Huldah Barksdale consort of W(N) G. Barksdale dau. of William and Selah Cannon Feb. 5, 1826-Aug. 14, 1854

George W. son of W.M. and Selah Cannon native of S.C. b. Feb. 18, 1806-Aug. 26, 1939

William Cannon b. in Tenn. Dec. 10, 1997. He emigrated to S.C. with his father when very young. Died in Miss. Oct. 5, 1843.

Selah consort of William Cannon b. S.C. June 15, 1786-died Nov. 30, 1840

William K. Austin d. June 1852 aged 26 yrs.

Benjamin Cannan son of Wm. & Selah Cannan b. S.C. Sept. 9, 1802-d. Kemper co. Aug. 17, 1850.

William Dozier son of Daxeus and Elizabeth Dozier b. Aug. 20, 1844-Aug. 2, 1850

Matthew Jackson b. 1797-d. Jan. 18, 1853

Janel Jackson b. 1797-Jan. 15, 1855 age 58

Franklin Thurmond d. Sept. 19, 1841 in 8th yr.

Fielding L. Thurmond d. Sept. 9, 1841 in 6th yr. Children of T.R. and Ann E. Thurmond.

James T. Whitsett d. May 11, 1857 41 yrs. 4 mo. 10 da.

Miss Mary E. Stewart 1843-1916

Joseph Stewart 1840-1908

Robert Jackson b. 1802-d. 1839 age 37

BIENSVILLE, MISS. CEMETERY

Wallace Lee Aust July 12,1881 – Dec.12,1908

Mary Ann Aust. Sept.4,1842 – Apr.24,1924

Nettie M. Aust Whittle June 4,1876 – Dec.2,1951

Samuel J. Aust 1862 – 1917

Louis Aust 1882 – 1931

Lerow Aust

Florence Aust wife of J.E.McCaskill July 5,1875 June 4,1928

John E. McCaskill Aug. 30,1872 – May 10,1914

Thomas J. Aust 1850 – 1902

J. Carroll Aust 1862 – 1934

Waldo Bryan Aug. 8,1912

Cornelia Evans Aust May 19,1852 – Nov. 23,1920

Nannie Dooly 1885 – 1942

Sallie S. Dooly 1861 – 1941(Mother)

Henery C. Dooly 1851 – 1905 (Father)

Henry Clay Dooly Mar. 20,1888 – Feb.10,1948

Mary Dooly 1877 – 1928

Dillard G. Dooly 1881 – 1936

Husband – Thomas C. Reynolds 1866-1943
Wife-Willie Dooly Reynolds 1881-1942

Wm. Inf.son of G.M.and A.M.Dial Apr. 7,1915 d. Dec.24,1915

Eller Donal wife of R.R.Boyd July 6,1862 May 18,1915

James Denton Dec. 28,1848 – Dec.29,1903

Sallie E. Denton wife Sept. 17,1857 – Sept. 1,1928

Margie Lee wife of J.W.Eaves Feb. 20,1879 – Apr.5,1906

Thomas Hill son of M. and A. Evans July 7,1910 – Sept 9,1911

Melbourn Evans Dec. 1,1884 – Dec. 15,1913

Sam   H.   Evans   1860–1942(**Ray's   uncle   by   marriage)

Ellen H. Evans 1861–1951 **(Miss Onie Hilbreth's sister. Ray's aunt)

Inf.   daughter   Guy   and   Mary   Kate   Cammack   Oct.21,1925

George W. Brown. Jan. 7,1897–Dec. 6,1950 Miss. Sgt.11 Inf 5 Division World War I

Byrd, son of Walter and F.L.Eaves

Mary Etheridge

Mary M. Etheridge wife of W.C. or G. Stuart May 2,1842 Dec. 10,1876 at church. wife, Walter and friend.

Henery A. Gay 1853–1932

Rebecca R. Gay 1856–1929

Amanda C. Joiner wife of R.L. Gilbert 1850–1936

R.L. Gilbert Dec. 18, 1844-Oct. 6, 1903

J.D.Honeycutt 1881–1914

Arthur M. Ingram Apr. 27,1850–June 20,1927

Lillie B. Ingram Aug. 8,1868–Jan. 12,1951

Mary Jones dau. J.O. and M.A. Aust b. Oct. 16,1886 d. Aug. 18,1901

Irma Irene Kitchens Feb. 18,1914–May 15,1916

Thomas J. Kitchens**(no dates) Co. B. 35 Miss. Inf. CSA.

Lucy Kitchens June 8, 1862-Oct. 5, 1919

Clyde W. Kitchens June 23, 1894-Dec. 31, 1916

Mother-Mattie P. Kitchens Feb. 22, 1858-Jan. 18, 1945
Father   "   (Mar. 30, 1854-Mar. 19, 1938

Father Ernest Kitchens Apr. 9, 1892-Aug. 27, 1944

Frances E. wife of W.L.Locke June 23, 1833-June 29, 1903

W.L.Locke Dec. 25, 1834-Apr. 6, 1919

Papa. Wm.H. Lavendar Aug. 8, 1865-Jan. 10, 1929
Mama Georgia E. Lavendar Feb. 28, 1869-Dec. 17, 1932

Lonnie Clyde Lavendar   husband.

Claudie H.Lavendar 1889-1918

Leon Gunter inf. son H. and G.E. Lavendar Nov. 22, 1898-Dec. 14, 1898

W.U.Lavendar Feb. 18, 1830-Jan. 15, 1898

Mary,   wife   of   W.U.Lavendar   May   7,   18320   Feb.   18,   1887

Wallace Bennett Lavendar 1920-1941

Mother Lula Lavendar wife of W.T. Boyd July 12, 1870-Jan. 14, 1942

Rev. Ford Newsom 1868-1889

Annie   Rutle   wife   of   C.B.Neel   Apr.   5,   1888-Feb.   7,   1918.

A.B.Lozier 1856-1923

Ida. Lozier 1859-1923

Father   Nicholas   C.Neel   b.   Sept.   18,   1852   d.Oct.   23,   1928

Georgia Apr. 15, 1856-Nov. 20, 1944

Leroy Jackson Honeycutt 1852-1888

James Moss 1850-1881

J.W.Jackson May 18, 1861-Dec. 14, 1897

Eula Smith Milsted Nov. 14, 1896-May 9,1926

Luther Milsted World War I Vet.*(Tomb broken)

Oscar Parnell Aug. 15, 1906-Apr. 24, 1938

Willie R. Parnell Jan. 10, 1857-Feb. 22, 1912

Willie Ann Parnell b. Feb. 5, 1870 d. July 24, 1953

Bettie McBryde Dec. 9, 1845-June 23, 1898

W.L.Ridgway Dec. 19, 1859-Junly 9, 1906

Sephalow Ridgway Oct. 25, 1864-Oct. 13, 1913

Mary Evelyn Neal Jan. 9, 1943-Jan. 11, 1943

William Harvey Oliphant Apr. 27, 1874 Feb. 8, 1939

Lucy B.dau.of Wm.H.and F.B.Oliphant Oct. 5, 1911-Feb. 10, 1927

Mamie Lois Snoddy Feb. 14, 1898-Dec. 9, 1920
(In Smith lot.)

Sam Smith 1880-1940

Tennie Barnett Smith 1876-1953

Jack Payne Aug. 13, 1897-1936

Father-Andrew Jackson Payne Jan. 8, 1859-Aug. 21, 1931
Mother   "   Aug. 23, 1969-Aug. 12, 1935

Willie S. Payne Ala. Wagr 104 Field Art. 39 Div. World War I July 1, 1895-Apr. 8, 1949

Paul Bradford Smith W. War I 140 Field Art. Miss. Mecles. 1895-1955

Wannie Louise Inf. Dau. J. T. and N. T. Stuart Apr. 25, 1909-May 23, 1909

(Clyde Jones Mother was a Lanier. Kin to Laniers and Bryants. Willia Sanders Jeremiah's brother M. Calloway)

Kate wife of C. T. Locke Oct 5, 1868-Dec. 9, 1919

Roger V. Parrish Missouri Pvt. 351 Inf. 88 Div. Oct. 4, 1918

John Lee Sparkman 1890-1905

Minnie M. Wife of A. M. Taylor Sept. 26, 1882-Apr. 29, 1903

James Calloway Warren (** Clyde's grandpa) Aug. 7, 1858-Feb. 23, 1954

Henry A. Warren (**son of James Calloway) Mar. 6, 1887-Nov. 5, 1927. Son Jack S. Warren **(grandson of James Callawy) July 17, 1923-Sept. 26, 1945

John T. Watt 1880-1943

Hattie Aust Watt 1887-1953* (Mamie's parents.)

J. J. Watt Co. K. 16 Cavalry

Caroline L. wife of J. J. Watt b. Apr. 29, 1845 Jan. 12, 1902

J. D. Ridgway July 30, 1861-Dec. 2, 1922
Mrs. Jeff   "   Nov. 24, 1848-June 19, 1938

Claude C. son of T. F. and A. A. Wiggins 1896-1900

Oscar Irving son of C. H. & M. E. Wiggins Mar. 12, 1889-Dec. 26, 1898

W. H. Stwart Feb. 7, 1807-Mar. 30, 1884

_____Williams (at church) Bienville Miss.

BROWNLEE CEMETERY
CEMETERY NEAR COLUMBUS, MISSISSIPPI

(On right of Hi-way between Columbus and Pickeyville)

James B. Brownlee Aug. 1, 1834- June 28, 1882

Evaline A. Brownlee May 3, 1850- aged 21 yrs.

David Brownlee d. May 24, 1850 aged 19 yrs.

Mary Brownlee June 7, 1832-aged 52

James Brownlee d. May 19, 1925 aged 50

Anna Brownlee d. Mar. 8, 1862

John Brownlee d. Apr. 24, 1862

James Brownlee d. Aug. 19, 1853

Col. Nimrod Davis d. Jan. 12, 1862

Wife of N.D. d. Aug. 12, 1844

Samuel A. Edmundson b. Camden S.C. 1794 d. Lowndes Co. Miss. 1869. "He won fame and the gratitude of our forefathers by his daring ride from Fort Stephens to Nashville Tenn. to procure Gen. Jackson's aid against the Creek Indians." Tablet presented by Bernard Romans Chapter D.A.R. Columbus, Miss 1926.

Mary Ann, wife of Lewis Green July 16, 1824-July 1, 1850

Rebecca wife of Samuel W. Lacey d. Dec. 31, 1851 aged 34

Inf. S.W. and R.A. Lacey

Drucilla Taggart Dec. 26, 1818 Jan. 22, 1851

Mary Taggart wife of Wm. Taggart d. July 23, 1858 in 75 yr.

Lt. Geo Norris

James Norris

John Norris

Joseph Norris age 2

Mary Norris

GILES CEMETERY NEAR SCOOBA, MISS.

Daniel W. Kerr 1832-1895

Peggy M. Jones wife of Daniel Kerr 1845-1915

A. Beverly Robinson 1883-1938

Mother, Laura K. Robinson 1854-1903

Father James B. Robinson d. Feb. 8, 1905

John B. Stuart Oct. 23, 1842-Dec. 26, 1915

J. T. Stuart Sept. 13, 1856-Jan. 18, 1926

Mary E. Stuart Feb. 24, 1858-Aug. 26, 1954

Annie Lee Stuart Nov. 25, 1879-Dec. 10, 1945

W. J. Vaughn Dec. 15, 1879-Oct. 21, 1908

Kitty May dau. of A. J. and S. P. Keen Dec. 6, 1887-Mar. 18, 1892

Simmons H. Giles Apr. 6, 1827-Sept. 3, 1870

Maria wife of Simmons H. Giles May 28, 1891 in 55th yr. **Formerly
Maria H. Jones

Jacob Giles July 27, 1799-Apr. 22, 1860

Our Mother Nancy wife of Jacob Giles d. Jan. 3, 1886 aged 85 yr. 1 mo.
10 da.

Charlottem Carr Oct. 24, 1818-Aug. 2, 1895

Pattie Winston Carr Carter d. Nov. 24, 1893 aged 34

Laura Evelyn Neville Apr. 18, 1875-Nov. 4, 1956

Albert Lindsey Neville Sept. 29, 1862-Nov. 17, 1911

Andrew L. Neville Feb. 29, 1848-Feb. 14, 1926

Mattie Evelyn Massey wife of Andrew L. Neville July 26, 1849-July 19,
1929

A. L. Neville June 29, 1815-Apr. 21, 1882

Nancy J. Neville Apr. 25, 1833-June 23, 1892

Shepherd Spencer Neville Jan. 7, 1920 in 62 yr **On cross: IHS

Maria Cross Giles Neville Feb. 20, 1859-Jan. 20, 1929 **On cross: IHS

Sara H. Spencer wife of W. H. Neville

Wm. H. son of William & E. L. Neville 1812-1887

Robert S. son of W. H. and Sara Neville 1849-1915

Helen N. Grant dau. of W. H. and Sara Neville 1856-1923

Martha Washington dau. of W. H. & Sara Neville 1862-1957

Mary Russell dau. of W. H. and Sara Neville 1864-1942

Mollie wife of W. H. Neville Jr.

Wm. McDow Neville d. 1881 aged 4 mo.

Perrin Neville d. 1882 aged 4 yrs.

Mollie wife of W. H. Neville Jr.

William Neville May 26, 1839-June 14, 1908

George M. Blocker Aug. 21, 1852-Aug. 29, 1901

Sallie Blocker Neville Nov. 1, 1848-Apr. 28, 1881

Conroe Simpson oldest child of W. T. and D. Coleman b. Jan. 4, 1873-June 19, 1885

Wiley T. Coleman July 16, 1840-Sept. 1, 1921

Mother Mary Ida wife of Wiley T. Coleman Mar. 20, 1856-Aug. 2, 1953

Husband Wiley Coleman Oct. 14, 1884-Dec. 8, 1945

William Dillon b. Old Wahallak Miss. Nov. 16, 1860 d. Welborn, Fla. Aug. 7, 1913

R. G. Dillon M. D. b. Dublin Ireland d. Noxubee Co. Miss. Apr. 2, 1897 aged 68 yrs.

Capt. T. U. Perrin Edgefield S. C. Sept. 23, 1832 d. New Orleans La. July 5, 1887

W. E. Pearson Jr. Feb. 1, 1869-July 2, 1937

Mary C. Pearson Mar. 14, 1874-Feb. 22, 1935

Dr. W. E. Pearson May 14, 1836-May 31, 1939

Cordelia wife of Dr. W. E. Pearson June 22, 1831 d. Nov. 30, 1907

John F. Pearson Sept. 22, 1866-Jan. 16, 1950

Mart Lacy Jan. 30, 1863-Sept. 2, 1896

Mary Florida Lacy Jones Perrin Apr. 26, 1841-Jan. 10, 1920

Sgt. Major William A. Perrin Co. C. Jeff Davis Legion CSA **Southern Cross

Father William B. Hare June 10, 1875-Jan. 9, 1928

Mother Sallie L. Hare Dec. 12, 1872-Jan. 9, 1947

Son Wm. Henry Hare apr. 2, 1896-Oct. 10, 1918

William Hervery Neville Nov. 12, 1812-July 25, 1887

Wife of Wm. Hervey Sarah H. Spencer Oct. 13, 1829-June 13, 1906

Children of Wm. Hervey & Sara H. Spencer.
1. Robert S. Neville Dec. 7, 1849-May 17, 1916
2. Helen Neville Grant Nov. 17, 1856-Jan. 14, 1923
3. Wm. Hervy Jr. Apr. 23, 1852-Nov. 14, 1922 and wife Amelia d. Mar. 10, 1929

**Cousin Ella Warren buried at New Hope Methodist Church near DeKalb, Miss.

Dixon Turner Oct. 1, 1820-Feb. 6, 1891

Margarat Turner June 9, 1829-April 20, 1912

Thomas W. Turner June 9, 1852-Dec. 11, 1887

John W. Turner July 17, 1838-Dec. 30, 1906

Benjamin Turner b. 1799-July 12, 1867

Albert E. Jackson Co. A. 11 Miss. Cav. CSA

B.T. Ashford b. Aug. 14, 1854-Sept. 18, 1923

**Ashfords and Castles related
   Bryans and Laniers near Scooba.
   Mrs. Bryan at cemetery near Scooba from Meridian

William Lanier m. Martha A. Bryan
1860 C-1 284 Greene Co.   **Marriage record

Robert Strait m. Mary Knox 1826

Boykin, Dr. Edwin D. 47
, Mary Gray 47
, Mary L. 47
, Martha A. 47
, N. A. 47
Bradford, Samuel T. 64
Bradley, Charley S. 43
Bragg, 34
Brantly, Janes 25, 27
Braune, Annie Theresa 38
, Gustave 38
, Honoria Theresa 38
Bray, Caswell 32
, Mary E. Ward 32
, Mattie Eloise 32
Breathwaite, James 23
Bridges, Angeline 58
, E. 58
, Edwin 58
, Harriet Jane 81
, John N. 58
, John W. 81
, Martha 58
, Sara A. 81
, William E. 58
Briggs, S. G. 48
, Thirza M. Cherry 48
Brockway, Capt. Benjamin Little 95
, Betty Lee 93
, C. I. 95
, W. G. 93
Brown, Annie D. 58
, B. W. 23
, Candice 58
, Caroline 59
, George W. 107
, Harriet 68
, H. Lee Sr. 26
, James 50
, James M. 58
, James W. 68, 85
, J. C. 85
, Jere Chapman 85
, J. M. 58
, John 58
, John G. 19
, Laura Irene 26
, M. A. 85
, Mary 58
, Mollie E. 24
, Peggy Jane 58
, S. C. 23

Brown, Lt. S. C. 34
, Stephen C. 24
, S. T. 59
, T. C. 58
, W. L. 15
, W. W. 23
, E. J. 73
Browne, F. F. 73
, Reavis Atherton 73
Brownlee, Andrew 12
, Anna 110
, David 110
, Evaline A. 110
, James 110
, James B. 110
, John 110
, Mary 110
, Sophie 12
, William S. 12
Brugh, Guy Pendleton 17
, Pendleton 17
Brumley, Susannah 42
Bryan, Catherine C. 15
, Martha A. 114
, William 15
Bullick, Eleanor Bretney 49
Buntin, J. W. 81
, Margaret V. 81
, Thomas C. 81
, Vincent 81
, William 81
Bunnell, Martha Ellen 66
, R. B. 64, 66
Burch, Samuel Joseph 17
Burglas, John 102
Burks, 34
Burnett, Mrs. L. M. 9
Burns, Elvira H. 87
, John H. 87
, Peter 23
, William Augustus 87
Burton, Ephraim T. 29
, Nancy 29
Bush, Adah 64
, A. T. 64
, Elias Hill 64
, M. A. 64
Byrd, Annie Thornton 17
, Catherine Marshall 17
, Daniel H. 18
, Susie Perry 18

Byrd, Taylor 18
Bryan, Elisha 15
    , T. 15
    , Waldo 106
    , William 15
    , Wm. T. 15
Cabeen, Elly 12
    , Thomas L. 12
Caldwell, John T. 41
    , R. J. 56
Calhoun, Agnes Long 12
    , Nancy Agnes 12
    , John C. 12
    , William 12
Calley, Sara 43
    , Martha Alice 43
    , W. P. 43
    , William 43
Calvin, Hiram 32
Cameron, Frankie 71
    , D. C. 71
    , Jimmie 71
    , Mary Ann 79
    , Nat 79
    , Nathaniel Allen 71
    , N. C. 71
    , N. D. 71
Campbell, Alexander 69
    , Daniel Love 63
    , David 56
    , Edward C. 35
    , Elizabeth D. 69
    , John 51
    , Mary 51, 57
    , Mary E. 63
    , Mary Esther Gorden 35
    , Robert 57
    , Samuel 57
    , W. M. Booth 63
Cammack, Guy 107
    , Mary Kate 107
Cannon, Benjamin 105
    , George W. 105
    , Selah 105
    , William 105
Carico, Elizabeth 70
Carnes, Amanda 51
    , Amelia 51, 53
    , Henry 51
    , Henry G. 51
    , Zilla 53
Carney, Clinton 40

Carney, Elise 40
    , John W. 40
    , L. A. 40
Carpenter, Alonzo Jefferson 103
    , Arthur H. 101
    , Churchwell 80
    , Eliza 22
    , Joel Pearson 45
    , John James 103
    , John Prince 38
    , J. R. 22
    , Kelly H. 96
    , Lillian Allman 37
    , M. A. 103
    , Malvina 80
    , Mary A. 80, 103
    , Mary G. 96
    , Mary M. 103, 104
    , M. M. A. 103
    , Minnie 96
    , Nancy K. 80
    , Capt. Nathan 34
    , S. T. 103
    , Samuel J. 37
    , Sidney C. 80
    , Simeon 103, 104
    , Willie C. 104
Carson, Mary Pickens 48
    , Moorehead 64
    , Thomas K. 48
Carr, Julia T. 93
    , Dr. P. E. 93
    , Paul Jr. 93
Carroll, Katie 46
    , W. G. 46
Cartee, Joseph 30
    , Sara Caroline 30
Carter, Pattie Winston 111
Carr, Charlotte 111
Cathron, Rev. B. E. 50
Chalmers, David W. 64
    , Martha J. 59
    , Mary Jane 64
    , Wm. 64
Chambers, J. M. 9
    , James M. 10
    , Rinie E. 9
    , Sara E. 10
Chapman, Alonzo B. 50
    , Euphemia 70
    , Mary Ann 77
    , John R. 103
    , Joseph 50

Chapman, Mary B. 103
    , Dr. Oscar 70
    , Simeon 36
    , W. C. 64
Chappell, H. B. Jr. 42, 43
    , Rosa Lee Dill 43
Cherry, Samuel T. 103
    , Sara 103
Childe, Amanda M. 72
Chiles, Betsy 86, 92
    , Emma 72
    , Judith Pollars 35
    , Mary H. 72
    , W. H. 72
    , Walter 35
Chotard, John Charles 8
Christian, Archer Hunt 49
    , Sallie 71
    , Sara Freeman 49
Clanton, Justinia Va. 13
    , Lucinda 46
    , Martha Louisa 46
    , Mary Elizabeth 46
    , Robert 46
    , Sylvia Jane 46
    , Temperance 46
Clay, James E. 103
Cleveland, Geo. 36
    , Jane B. 36
Clinton, Charles 50
    , Sara E. 24
Cluster, Capt. S. W. McAliley 22
Coats, Tempie B. 5
Cobb. David 10
    , James 36
    , John H. 36
    , Medora Steele 29
    , Nehemiah 10
    , Thomas William 29
Cochran, Willie Calvin 75
    , J. 23
    , M. Jane 20, 23
Cockrell, John 90
    , John William 98
    , Nancy 70
Colby, William M. 59
Cole, Capt. Geo. H. 34
    , L. B. 97
    , Malissa 97
    , Rhonda 97
Coleman, Augustus 14
    , Aquilla H. 14
    , Charles H. 14
    , Conroe Simpson 112
    , D. 112
    , Elizabeth M. 21

, Geo. K. 45
, Harriet Dunlap 32
, James C. 32
, Jessie B. W. 21
, Mary Ida 112
, Nancy A. 21
, Nancy 88
, Priscilla A. Hutton 14
, Capt. Thomas W. 34
, Thomas 100
, Wiley 112
, William 21
, Wiley T. 112
Colson, Gertrude 31
Colvin, Elizabeth 10
, Francis M. 19
, Hiram 35
, Isabella 75
, John Allen 75
, J. S. 75
, John Shackelford 75
, John Walter 78
, Mary 19
, Mary Anna 75
, Mary E. 35
, Mollie S. 35
, Sinthey E. 19
, Thomas 19
, William 78
, W. V. 87
Collier, G. W. 103
, M. C. 103
Collins, Alonzo 78
, Drucilla Eliza 51
, F. 51
, Fanny R. 85
, Hiram G. 6
, John J. 51
, M. 31
, Orlando 51
, Penelope 51
, Posey G. 51
, R. C. 31
, Willie 101
Cook, Annie M. 94
, Eula Bell 8
, James B. 24
, Laura E. 23
, Mary T. 24

Cook, Mary M. 8
, Mollie E. 23
, Stephen R. 8
, Dr. Stephen 8
, James Jack 25
, Mary Brown 64
Cooper, Rebecca 29
Constantine, C. C. 39
, Clementine C. 83
, Dr. F. L. 39
, Fannie A. 39
, Francis 39
, Francis L. 83
, Henry Lewis 83
Connor, Annie 93
, Sallie 93
Copp, Emma S. 36
Corwin, Mable 90
Cother, Elizabeth 80
, Jesse 80
Cottles, Wm. O. 103
Cox, Alfred B. 66
, Katie Mae 64
, Robert J. 64
, Wm. Walter 64
, Matilda C. 64
Crafts, Johnny Berts 87
Craig, Augusta Dwan 12
, Catherine C. 12
, Cornelia Jane 12
, James 12
, James Newton 12
, Robert 12, 15
, Marcellus Octabius 12
Crantham, Cora 70
Craven, Dr. J. P. 43
, Mary Lou 43
Crawford, Christine A. 9
, M. B. 9
, Capt. Robert 34
Creed, Joe 94
Crenshaw, Anderson 34
Crim, Jane 42
, Juli F. 102
, Dr. Thomas 42
, Warren W. 45
, W. W. 102
Crisell, Elijah 47
Cromwell, Mary G. 47
Cross, Mary 36
Crook, John W. 94

Crooks, Minnie 82
, S. F. 82
Crow, Walter Elmer 73
Cummings, Oliver T. 78
Cunningham, Catherine 38
, James 38
, John Francis 38
, Katie Louise 38
Churchwell, Harriet 80
Curtis, Elijah 4
, Sarah 4
, D. S. 64
, Mary A. 64
, Mary Pulham 64
Dabney, Margaret 84
Dabbins 28
Daley, J. Frank 38
, John 38
, Patrick 38
Dallas, Alexander Sr. 4
, Eliza 4
Dancy, Edwin C. 47
Dandridge, Rosa Sanford 16
Daniel, Arthur 44
, B. 44
, D. 44
, Geo. H. 44
, J. 44
, John 44
, Lula G. 44
, M. J. 44
, Marcus C. 44
, Penjnah 44
, Sarah E. 44
, Thomas 44
, William 44
Darden, Clemmon 47
Darrow, Bettie G. 82
Daugherty, Thomas 22
Davidson, F. 1
, Dr. Frank 2
, Helen M. 2
, John Henry 2
, Mollie Melton 1
, Sallie 1
Davitt, Wm. 23
Davis, A. Rand 19
, J. F. 26
, Leah 26
, Mary C. 10
, Col. Nimrod 110
, Sarah 88
, Savilla 19

Davis, Sophia 88
    , Thomas Colvin 19
    , Dr. Wm. 88
    , W. W. 10
Degraffenried, Anne Eliza 14
            , Celestia F. S. 14
            , Christipher M. 14
            , Elizabeth A. 14
            , John Calhoun 14
            , John F. 14
            , Rebecca C. Hill 14
            , Rebecca H. 14
            , Dr. T. 14
DeYampert, Niece Susan Brown 50
Demoville, A. B. 16
            , Isora Glover 16
            , John Fant 16
Denton, James 106
        , Sallie E. 106
Derryberry, C. W. 51
            , T. F. 51
Dew, Nannie Taylor 32
Dial, A. M. 106
    , G. M. 106
    , Wm. 106
Dillard, Benjamin 49
        , Geo. 28
        , Lydia 28
        , Marja J. Georgia 28
        , M. D. 112
        , William 112
Dimick, Nelson 85
Dobbins 28
Dodson, Joe 41
        , Mary Daisy 1
        , W. R. 1
Donal, Eller 106
Donaldson, Mary 59
Dooly, Dillard G. 106
        , Henry Clay 106
Dorsey, Annie A. 38
Dorroh, Bonnie 64
Doss, Henry James 101
        , Lyda 101
Douglas, Robert Bruce 48
Downing, James Samuel 5
Dozier, Daxeus 105
        , Eliiz. 105
        , William 105
Dolly, Mary 106
        , Nannie 106
        , Sallie S. 106

Drake, Eliza 64
    , Harriet Osborn 49
    , Hattie May 49
    , Mary Ethel 49
    , N. 64
    , Robert W. 49
Drummond, Margaret 10
Dugger, Bolling W. 49
        , Willie Hurt 49
Dunbar, William 8
Duncan, Dr. Augustus 34
Dunlap, Annie E. 22
        , E. A. 101
        , E. R. 101
        , Josiah C. 51
        , R. Bass 34
        , David R. 24
        , Elizabeth 24
        , Geo. H. 32, 35
        , James 31
        , James P. 22
        , John 24
        , Louisa 32, 35
        , Martha 22
        , Robt. 22
Duram, R. R. 57
Durham, J. M. 38
        , Margaret 38
        , Martha 38
Durrett. W. M. Brantley 30
Easley, Rev. Joseph W. 66
Easton, Alice 101
Eaton, Alice M. 72
      , T. 72
Eatman, Augusta May 32
        , Caroline 28
        , Cornelis 30
        , Elizabeth 28
        , G. I. 59
        , H. F. 72
        , H. G. 32
        , Irving 28
        , Jethro B. 28
        , John 28
        , Judith Taylor 28
        , M. A. 59
        , Mary 28
        , Redding 28
        , Ross V. 59
        , Sarah 28
        , Sedan S. 30
        , William 28, 54
        , W. B. 28

Fulton, Dr. James S. 27
, Louisa M. Glenn 27
, Mary Bell 46
, Paul 46
, R. C. 56
, S. H. C. 56
, Simeon 59
Gabriel, Dr. 20
Gammill, Melissa Caroline 59
, Samuel Maxwell 59
, W. M. 59
Gandy, Aphis Omega 3
, Buster 3
Garland, James P. 77
Garner, Mary A. 68
, Starling 68
Garnet, J. 50
Garth, Fannie Adams 44
, Nimrod Garland Sr. 84
Gass, W. M. 21
Gaston, Elizabeth 4
, Hugh 4
, Wm. 4
Gay, Ben 44
, Delphia 44
, Henry A. 107
, Rebecca 107
, Wallace 44
, Willie J. 44
Geiger, Belle Houston 45
, Capt. A. 44
, C. B. 45
, J. C. 45
, Wm. M. 45
Gentry, J. W. 45
George, James C. 15
, James G. 15
, Matilda 28
, Nancy Wilmouth 5
, Panela E. 8
, Permela E. 15
Gewin, Emerett Ferrell 77
, Capt. Noah Hampton 77
, Mary Ann 77
Gibson, Thad 87
Gilbert, R. L. 107
Giles, Jacob 111
, Maria 111
, Nancy J. 111
, Simmons H. 111
Gill, James 23

Gill, Mary A. 23
, M. Willie 47
, Nancy 23
, Robert 23
Gillespie, Adell 2
, John 10
, Lydia P. 10
, Mary McKee 5
, Marion 2
Gilbert, Rhoda 42
Gladney, David 74
Glass, R. W. L. 64
Glenn, Nancy 27
, Simeon 27
Glover, Alfren Young 40
, Antoinette Malone 40
, Cato D. 40
, Cornelia Bevill 40
Green, Lewis 110
, Mary Ann 110
Glover, Emma Dephine Seed 40
, Emma S. 40
, Mary Sophie 40
, Sara Va. 40
, Thomas L. 40
, Williamson 40
Godfrey, Julia Augusta 46
Goehner, Hannah Christina 75
Goodlaw, French S. 21
Gordon, Adeline 52
, Anna 31
, Anna S. 22
, Anne E. 23
, Annie G. 36
, Benjamin F. 36
, Berry H. 80
, Chas. E. 23
, Edward E. 23
, Elizabeth 51
, Elizabeth S. 51
, Fanny 24
, Fred A. 31
, F. S. 22
, Gulnair Adelkiza 52
, J. 47
, Jefferson 47, 52
, Jesse Sr. 52
, Lycurgus 52
, Maria 80
, M. C. 47
, McGregor Mary Ann 36

Hamlett, Wm. A. 37, 39
    , W. R. 39
    , Willis C. 37
Hammond, Martha 85
Hanley, Rev. L. S. 22
    , Sallie Clara 22
Hanna, Andrew 77
    , Martha J. 77
    , R. C. 77
    , R. G. 78
    , Robert 77
Harding, Eliza 8
Hardman, H. Dunn 64
Harlan, Matie H. 17
Harper, A. E. 2
    , C. C. 4
    , James 82
    , Sophie 1
    , J. W. 1
    , Wm. J. 1, 2
    , Wyatt 1
    , Z. C. 2
Harshall, Wm. Henry 42
Hartsfield, Ella Maude 6
    , James M. 6
    , Mabel Louisa 6
    , S. E. 6
Harvey, Martha 51
Hatch, A. 49
    , E. 49
Hatter, Kate 22
    , Katherine 8
    , Nancy Jane 20
    , Richard B. 49
    , Richard N. 11
    , Sallie A. Hutton 11
    , W. R. 8
    , W. R. B. 22
Hayley, Annie Ling Little 45
    , John A. 45
Haywood, Dr. William D. 48
Hardy, E. E. 104
    , E. W. 25
    , Edwin-Covington 37, 39
    , Mary 104
    , Stith 63
    , Will 14
Hare, John 94
    , Martha H. 94
    , Sallie L. 113
    , William B. 113
    , Wm. Henry 113

Harris, Ann 62
    , A. H. 85
    , Catherine 62
    , Dorcas 62
    , Elizabeth 80
    , Elizabeth A 62
    , Eliz. P. 62
    , Geo. 63
    , Harriet Louisa 63
    , Hester Ann 77
    , Hudson 80
    , Hugh M. 62
    , James G. 63
    , Joseph H. 62
    , Josiah 80
    , John F. 77
    , John S. 62
    , Laban H. 80
    , M. W. 85
    , Mary 63
    , Mary A. 63
    , Mary Ann Minerva 80
    , O. S. 80, 82
    , Owen S. 80, 82
    , Polly 80
    , Polly B. Ricks 80, 82
    , Sara Ricks 80
    , S. W. 80
    , Tilman M. 80
    , W. A. 80
Harrison, Anna 54
    , Bettie 82
    , Jethro 54
    , Mary 54
    , Sally 82
    , Temperance 28, 82
    , Wm. 28, 82
Harry, Mary Leila Borden 25
    , S. F. 25
    , Wm. Howell 31
Head, James 49
Henderson, Charlotte C. 4, 6
    , Elizabeth 33
    , E. W. 10
    , John D. 33
    , Lewis 4, 5, 6
    , Lewis W. 6
    , Obedience 5
    , Sara 4
    , Wm. F. 6
Henley, Albert T. 101
    , Sara 101

Herndon, Harry Talmin 36
   , Thos. H. 36
Hibbler, J. L. 95
   , M. A. 95
   , Martha Blount 95
   , Robert 95
Hickman, Geo. M. 32
Hicks, Grady R. 100
Higginbotham, Benj. T. 24
      , Maj. Geo 22
      , Major Geo. G. 24
      , Mary Va. 24
      , Sallie 24
Hilbreths, Onie 107
      , Rev. Sardine 101
Hill, Albert C. 32
   , C. Rebecca 14
   , E. E. 37
   , Elizabeth E. 37
   , Gabriel D. 37
   , Gabriel L. 37
   , Geo. W. 13
   , John Moore 13
   , Mary C. Bray 32
   , Mary E. 37
   , Moses 13
   , Pleasant 102
   , R. W. 39
   , Robert W. 37
   , Sara A. 13
   , Sevilla N. Roden 13
   , S. J. 37
   , Thomas Jefferson 13
   , William Judge 13
Hilman, Judson J. 5
      , L. A. 5
      , N. 5
Hines, Joseph B. 64
Holcroft, John W. 41
      , Nannie J. 41
      , Rebecca 41
Holmes, Martin 64
Holland, Sara 59
Holly, D. 43
   , Martha 43
   , Reeder 29
Holyfield, Daniel 3
Honeycutt, J. D. 107
Hopking, S. H. 80, 91
      , Faniel 101
      , Lucien Douglas 48

Hopkins, M. 48
   , Martha 80, 91
   , Mary E. 104
   , R. 48
Hopping, Phoebe 101
Horn, 34
Holston, C. A. 57
   , J. W. 57
Honeycutt. Leroy Jackson 108
Horton, A. S. 55
   , Cornelia 101
   , Elizabeth 1
   , Frances S. A. 1
   , G. A. 55
   , Harriet 29
   , J. A. 55
   , James W. 55
   , Jesse 55
   , Jesse Habbord 55
   , John D. 55
   , Julia 55
   , Lewis Dunkin 55
   , M. M. 55
   , Marcia L. 55
   , Margaret Ann 1
   , Mary 55
   , Ophelia 81
   , Sara 55
   , Sara R. 55
   , Stephen 1
   , Wm. H. 101
   , W. M. 55
   , William 55
Houston, Adell Grove 46
   , Almira S. 46
   , Anna M. 46
   , Jack 46
   , John J. 46
   , R. L. 46
   , A. W. 36
Hutt, Josephine H. 56
Huff, Rencher Louisa 33
   , Wm. 33
Hughes Andrew B. 101
   , James G. 59
   , Sallie B. 101
   , Col. Joseph 59
Huggins, Dr. Burrell 12
Huldah, Jeanie 18
Hutchins, James L. 72
      , Mary 49

Hutchins, Sara R. 72
Holland, Jacob 59
Hunt, Archer 50
Hunter, Mary A. 24
    , Robert O. 24
Hunnicut, John A. 45
    , Fannie 45
Hutton, Adon Cornelia 11
    , A. D. 38
    , Allen 69
    , Alonzo 11
    , Ann 22
    , Aquilla 69
    , Aquilla D. M. D. 11
    , Augustus G.
    , Catherine C. 15
    , Rev. C. M. 100
    , E. J. 11
    , Edward 69
    , Eliza 11
    , Elizabeth H. 11
    , Francis M. Fr. 69
    , Francis Marion 69, 100
    , John A. 11
    , John Newton 11, 69
    , Joseph 22, 100
    , Joseph A. 11
    , Katherine 8
    , Leonidas 22
    , General Joseph 12, 69
    , Nancy Agnes Calhoun 69, 100
    , Nancy Calhoun 12, 22
    , Permela 15
    , Sarah Hellen 69
    , Wm. J. 22
    , Wm. Joseph 100
    , Wm. Josephus 22
Hylton, Thomas Sterling 16

Inge, Annie Brown 32, 35
    , Frank 32, 35
Ingram, Arthur M. 107
    , J. M. 64
    , Lillie B. 107
    , P. 64
    , Maggie 70
Jack, Ann S. 27
    , James 25, 27
    , Mary Julia Witherspoon 25

Jack, Patrick Houston 26
    , Wm. Spencer Jr. 48
Jackson, Albert E. 114
    , Henry M. 72
    , Janel
    , J. W. 108
    , Matthew 105
    , Robert 105
Janes, Peggy M. 110
Jenkins, J. T. 93, 96
    , Mary L. 93
Jemison, Gertrude 64
Jennings, John Benjamin 98
Jeter, C. H. 41
    , Litius 41
Joiner, Amanda C. 107
Jolly, Arnals 22
    , Aura G. 52
    , J. W. 22
    , Judith W. 52
Jolly, Dr. M. A. 52
    , Prnold 52
Jones, Maria H. 111
Jordon, Ann 50
    , Fannie L. 59
Johnson, John 88
    , John C. 104
    , J. V. 59
    , Martha A. 88
    , Mary M. A. 103
    , M. E. 59
    , Oliver B. 59
    , Sarah 88
Johnston, Joseph E. 58
    , Mary Arrington 16
    , Mildred 64
    , Robt. 64
    , Samuel Harrison 16

    , Sara Emily 64
Jones, Adam 98
    , Alford 98
    , Alfred 42
    , Allen C. 48
    , A. P. 57
    , Catherine Erwin 48
    , Clyde 29
    , Elizabeth Jane Pearre 26
    , Guesner P. 82
    , James 26

Jones, Joel Winston 35
    , John Erwin 48
    , John Randolph 26
    , Lula 98
    , Martha Alice 26
    , Mary 107
    , Pearie H. 82
    , Pearre Howard 82
    , Pickney 57
    , Robert Jones 26
    , Stephen 66
    , Taniariah 57
    , Wm. E. 21
    , Wm. M. 26
Keeler, Alfred 81
Keen, A. J. 111
    , Kitty May 111
    , S. P. 111
Kelly, Gershom 64
Kelley, Hinton R. 59
    , John 38
    , Nancy A. 59
    , Sary 59
Kemp, Mary E. 64
Kemmedy, Elizabeth M. 20
    , James M. 100
    , Lawrence Richard 26
    , Maude Heddleston 27
    , Robert K. 27
    , Rev. Robert W. B. 59
    , Sanders 78
    , Thomas Brandon 20
Kerr, Daniel W. 111
Kilpatrick, Joseph 98
Kimble, Isham 83
Kimmbrough, James D. 75
    , M. E. 75
King, Berry 55
    , Bessie Adams 44
    , J. M. 74
    , M. B. 74
Kirkland, Elizabeth B. 12
    , Isaac 12
    , Mary 12, 15
    , Mattie 15
King, Molsey 55
Kitchens, Clyde W. 107
    , Ernest 107
    , Irma Irene 107

Kitchens, Lucy 107
    , Mattie P. 107
    , Thomas J. 107
Kittenberry, N. B. 96
    , Ollie Atkins 96
Knight, Wm. L. 97
Knox, Carolina 75
    , James M. 74
    , Jane 75
    , Mary 114
    , Matthew 75
Leslie, Fannie 18
    , R. H. 18
Levett, Dr. J. D. K. 50
Lewis, A. C. 30
    , Cornelia Ann 41
    , James 41
    , James Gaston 41
    , Malisa 30
Lewiston, Mary Julia
    , Middleton 28
Lewis, Nancy 41
Lightfoot, Dr. Phillip Lewis 33
    , Harriet Brown 33
    , Isabella Drummons 33
Limpscome, Joel 86
    , Joel 92
    , J. Powel 92
Little, Blake 46
    , Charles Henry 94
    , E. S. 96
    , Harriet S. 95
    , J. J. 45
    , Laura J. 95
    , Lucie P. 47
    , Maggie 96
    , Margaret E. 95
    , Mary 45, 46
    , Mary Elizabeth 93, 94
    , Nancy 95
    , Noah 94
    , Sara 45
    , Seth 95
    , Seth S. 93, 94
    , Tempy 95
    , Wm. 95
    , Dr. W. G. 47
    , Wm. G. Jr. 95, 96

Lyon, L. L. 67
  , Lude 90
  , Martha 67
  , Mary F. 67
  , Mary J. 67
  , Richard L. 67
  , Susan 46
  , Thomas H. 67
  , Wm. B. 67
Mabry, A. G. 104
  , Emmet A. 96
  , E. T. 9
  , Frances 21
  , Jesse G. 96
  , Jesse Peebles 96
  , Robert E. 9
Mackey, C. F. 56
  , E. B. 56
MacLemore, Annie Burt 8
  , Wilkes C. 8
Mariah, Della 22
Marshall, Ann 42
  , Elinor Ford 18
  , Lucille Ann 18
  , Martha E. 18
  , Mary Ford 18
  , Mildred Mae 18
  , Robert 20
  , DS. M. 18
  , Samuel Marvin Jr. 18
  , Wesley 42
Marriott, Aley J. 91
  , Ida Rice 91
Mason, Catheron E. K. 82
Massey, Kate 52
Madison, James A. 56
  , Narcilla 56
Malone, Margaret F. 35
Mann, Benjamin H. 83
Marine, B. W. 97
  , Maude 97
Marion, 82
Marriott, Benjamin 91
  , James W. 91
  , Mary A. 91
  , Samuel 91
  , Samuel R. 80
Mason, Henry S. 82
Maxwell, Elizabeth 23, 24
  , Elivra H. 87
  , Simeon 24

Maxwell, Col. Simeon 23
May, Albert J. 86, 92
  , A. P. 92
  , Francis Taylor 86
  , James H. 33
  , James M. 33
  , Jeanie Elizabeth 33
  , Kate R. 33
  , T. T. 92
  , Thaddeus Theodore 86
  , Wm. 1
Mays, Martha Nancy 61
  , Joseph 60
  , Louise L. 60
  , Mrs. Rachel A. 61
  , Dr. WM. 61
Mayo, Sara A. 75
McAlpine, Bradley Ridgeway 16
  , John W. 34
  , Mary Ridgeway 16
  , Sara Pritchett 16
  , Winston 16
McAllister, Wm. 6
McBryde, Bettie 108
McCaskill, John E. 106
McClinton, Elizabeth 40
McCracken, Charley 60
  , Cyrus 61
  , Jane 74
  , John G. 74
  , L. A. 60
  , Lydia 74
  , S. J. 60
  , Susan 61
  , Wm. 35
  , W. M. 61
  , William 74
McCrory, Catherine 81
  , James 81
  , James M. 81
  , Jane 81
  , Robert 81
  , Dr. William 57
McCulley, Lydia Whittaker 68
McCurdy, Oliver Moore 3
McDonald, Allen 69
  , Sarah 69
  , William 83
McDow, Arthur 20
  , Margaret 20
McFarland, Lucy 5

McGehee, Dabney 75
        , John P. 64
        , Nancy E. 64
McGiffert, Annie 74
        , David 74
        , Mary 74
        , Mary J. 74
McGowin, Della 11
        , Geo. Hill 11
        , John S. 11
        , Lue Hill 96
McGraw, Martha 9
        , S. D. 9
McGregor, J. G. 36
McIntosh 34
McKane, Alexander 57
        , Sara 57
McKee, Eliza C. 2
        , J. 18
        , William 2
McKeemie, Robt. 27, 26
        , S. H. 26
        , Susannah 27
McKennie, Thomas Francis 26
McKinley, John 38
        , Margaret Augustus 38
McLain, E. A. 37
        , H. R. 37
        , Tellitha 37
McMahon, A. W. 72
        , Mattie 72
        , Col. R. G. 84
McTurk, Isabella 84
Milner, Caroline E. 21
        , James Ed. 21
        , J. S. 21
Mills, Bertha Thaxton 98
Miller, Charles 23
        , Charles H. 20
        , Harry W. 23
        , James W. 60
        , John J. 23
        , Kate G. 23, 60
        , Linda 60
        , Malinda 60
        , M. E. 48
        , Robert Hindaman 60
        , S. P. 48
        , Sara T. 20, 23
        , W. G. 48
        , Wm. H. 23, 60
        , WM. 60
        , W. O. 48

Milsted, Eula Smith 108
        , Luther 198
Minor, Dabney 84
        , Eliza Perry 16
        , Dr. P. B. 16
        , Dr. John L. 17
        , Philip Barbour 17
Mitchell, Daniel 84
        , James 84
        , Martha Augustus 84
        , Mary 28
        , W. B. 28
Mixon, Janne 81
Mize, John T. 30
        , Kate 30
        , Willie Elbert 30
        , Wm. Samuel 30
Mobley, Bob 70
        , C. C. 69
        , Columbus C. 69
        , Christopher Columbus (Lum) 70
        , Constantine 70
        , D. C. (Dewitt) 69
        , Eugene 70
        , Greene B. 70, 72
        , Imogene 70
        , Irving 70
        , Isarah 70
        , John Bird 69
        , Lizzie 70, 103
        , Mary 69
        , Mary A. E. 69
        , R. E. Sr. 69
        , Rad E. Sr. 69
        , Rad (Ellis) 70
        , Robert (Bob) 70
        , Shelton 70
        , W. A. (Mike) 70
        , Wiley 70
Molinelli, Joseph 38
Monchief, Sophia 5
Monett, Rev. James 83
Moss, James 108
Moten, Eliza 20
Moore, Amanda M. 49
        , Dr. A. M. 50
        , Lt. Alfred M. 49
        , John Wilson 98
        , R. L. 61
        , Susie Weston 97
        , Sydenham 49
        , Col. Sydenham 49, 50
        , Thomas D. 97

Moore, Thomas Oliver 97
    , WM. 60
    , Weston 97
    , Wm. Webb 49
Mooring, F. G. 22
    , J. A. 72
    , Julia A. 72
    , Martha 72
Morgan, Barbara 46
    , Frank Grove 95
    , H. A. 95
    , Isabel 3
    , John 46
    , Marion T. 69
    , Mary G. 69
    , Mollie B. 95
    , Sara 46
    , Thomas A. 69
    , Dr. W. W. 3
Morris, AAron 66
Morrow, A. L. 61
    , Catherine 61
    , J. N. 29
    , Margaret E. 29
Mullins, Eliz. 68
    , John R. 68
    , Missouri Jackson 68
Munchief, Frances 5
    , Sampson 5
Munda, F. H. 32
Murphy, V. C. 35
Murray, John 4
Mushn, Janie B. 82
Muslin, Janie B. 82
Meador, Job. 6
Meadows, James Ross 60
    , M. G. 60
    , Margaret Opella 61
    , W. M. 60
Means, Delia Thornton 17
    , John David 17
Meek, Capt. James T. 44
    , John McCaw 45
    , Rosa Little 45
Melton, Ann 82, 86, 92
    , Bartlett Rev. 1
    , Bascom 4
    , C. C. 1
    , Ella Thomas 1
    , J. J. 5
    , L. E. 5
    , Mary1
    , Robert W. 5
    , Wm. A. 92
    , Wm. L. 4

Meredith, Ann Eliza 73
    , R. 73
Meriwether, Fred 34
    , Dr. John S. 35
    , Reuben A. 73
    , Dr. Willis 35
    , Willis 34
Metcalf, Jocob R. 72
    , Sophie E. 72

Nance, Avarilla 72
    , James Walter 72
    , Sarah 72
    , Wm. H. 72
    , W. T. 72
Nash, C. E. 47
    , Caroline Fay 47
    , Ida M. 47
    , James J. 46
    , M. J. 46
    , S. E. 46, 47
    , Stanton 22
    , Stephen 47
    , Stephen E. 22
Neal, E. T. 96
    , James 96
    , Mary Evelyn 108
    , T. P. 96, 97
Neil Geo. R. 103
    , Neal Ernest 103
Neel, Annie Rutle 108
    , C. B. 108
    , Nicholas C. 108
Nelson, Rebecca Jones 48
Neilson, G. A. 96
    , G. F. 96
    , Howard Rogers 96
Nesmith, Margaret 26
Neville, A. L. 111
    , Andrew L. 111
    , E. L. 112
    , Helen N. Grant 112
    , Laura Evelyn 111
    , Maria Cross Giles 111
    , Mary Russell 102
    , Martha Washington 112
    , Mattie Evelyn 111
    , Mollie 112
    , Nancy J. 111
    , Perrin 112
    , Robert S. 112
    , Shephert Spencer 111
    , William 112
    , William Harvery 113
    , Wm. McDow 112

Powers, Julia 26
Powell, Luella 46
       , R. W. 46
       , Temperance 3
Price, T. J. 31
Pritchett, Bettie Jackson 16
          , James 16
Prreck, John C. 50
Prude, William 98
      , Z. K. 98
Pullis, T. R. 82
Quarles, C. M. 96
        , Minnie Windham 96
Quitman, Mary 50
Ragsdale, Geo I. 64
         , Hiram C. 84
         , Mary 70
         , Virena 84
         , Wesley 104
Rea, Louisa C. 104
   , Louisa A. 104
   , Mary 88
   , John L. 104
Reavis, Robert 85
Rencher, David G. 33
        , Elizabeth 4
Reid, Pricilla 94
    , Robert 94
Ren, Eliza Jane 88
   , Marshall 88
Rens, William Willoughby 16
Reynolds, Marvin 10
         , Thomas C. 106
         , Willie Dooly 106
Rhoden, Alexander L. 97
Rhodes, Alvin 50
       , Annie B. 30
       , Elmira Jane 61
       , Emerson Perry 38
       , James 61
       , John W. 30
       , M. J. 30
       , Pressley R. 30
       , T. M. 50
       , W. E. 30
Rice, Aley A. 91
    , Alexander C. 91
    , E. G. 56
    , Ella Lavendar 56
    , Frank 91
    , Hopking 91

, Jane 91
, J. P. 52
, John P. 50
, M. J. 57
, Mary Irene 57
, Neverson 91
, Pinckney 27
, W. D. 91
Richard, Elizabeth 24
       , Wm. 24
Richardson, Carrie 4
          , Elizabeth 100
          , Frank 4
          , J. M. 56
          , Luka 4
          , Sally N (W) 100
          , Willie 56
          , Wm. 100
Richey, Mary A. 10
Richmand, Evelyn Wilson 26
        , N. T. 26
Ridgway, J. D. 109
        , Jeff 109
        , Mary 33
        , S. 33
        , Sephalow 108
        , W. L. 108
Rockbridge, Col. John McKee 8
Roberts, Mamie Boyd 38
        , S. W. 38
Robinson, A. Beverly 111
         , Eliz. 104
         , James 111
         , Laura K. 111
         , Ruth J. 36
Roden, Delia 36
     , James 31
     , Sara Dunlap 31
Roebuck, Louise 21
        , Mary 29
Rogers, A. A. 45
       , Annie E. 94, 104
       , C. M. A. 94
       , H. G. 61
       , James L. 44
       , Jane 44
       , Jane Caroline 44
       , L. 61
       , James Pinchkney 93
       , Joseph 44
       , Lucy A. 44

Rogers, Martha Wliza 44
  , Mary M. M. A. 104
  , Redmon 44
  , Sara A. 45
  , Sallie E. 96
  , Sophia Gray 93
  , Tabitha 44
  , T. H. 104
  , Thos. H. 23
  , Va. Hannah 45
  , Wm. 44
  , Wm. R. 64
Ross, Capt. Walter R. 27
Rowston, Col. Young L. 83
Rurnell, Rufie 90
Rushing, America 2
  , American E. 6
  , Christopher C. 3
  , Elizabeth 3
  , James 3
  , J. M. 3, 5, 6
  , Laura 5
  , Lorenzo 5
  , Leonidas 2
  , Marshall B. 3
  , Mary 2
  , Shepherd 1
  , Susan 3, 5
  , Susannah 5
  , Winston 2
Rutledge, Isaac 15
  , Aunt Laura 15
  , Wm. 15
Ryam, C. E. 56
Sanders, Charley Peak 70
  , Edward C. 73
  , H. J. 22
  , Rebecca S. 13
  , S. H. 22
Savage, Rebecca 51
Scales, Ruth 29
Scarbrough, J. W. 55
  , Martha 44
  , N. J. 55
  , Wm. 32
  , wm. R. 55
Scott, John M. D. 72
Seed, A. W. 50
  , C. C. 50
Seibert, J. Nickel 4
  , John 4
  , William 4

Selden, R. G. M. 35
Sellars, Elijah 30
  , Nancy J. 30
Shait, Eliza 21
  , James 21
  , Margaret 21
  , Walter Scott 21
Shattuck, Blanch 17
Shaver, Caroline 47
  , Rev. O. H. 47
Shaw, Christopher 24
  , Mary Helen 20
Sheffield, John 3
Shelton, An 32
  , A. N. 37
  , May 32
  , May I 37
Shephard, Mary Moorehead 68
  , Wm. Paschal 68
Sherrod, Elizabeth 42
  , Jane E. Bonner
  , Sandall 42
Shotwell, James L. 64
  , Mora Ann 64
Skinner, Elizabeth 25
Slaughter, John M. 80
  , Susan L. 80
Sims, James 51, 104
  , Lasey 104
Simmons, David S. 96
  , Rhoda 26
Simpson, Charlotte 60
Singley, Georgia 56
Singleton, Richardson 104
Smaw, Annie H. 17
  , S. B. 17
Smith, Dr. A. H. 84
  , Adella 5
  , Albert 10
  , Albert Henry 84
  , Rev. Albert M. 10
  , Annie M. 10, 19
  , B. F. 53
  , C. E. 6
  , D. Kimbrough 9
  , D. W. W. 53
  , Delida 32
  , E. Kirby 9
  , Elizabeth 53
  , Eula Lee 19
  , Florence T. 9
  , Geo. 32

Smith, Geo. Washington 10
, Harriet Harris 73
, Rev. Israel G. 31
, J. F. 53
, Dr. J. J. 19
, Rev. M. P. 10
, James H. 53
, Jennie Perrin 31
, John A. 9
, John C. 31
, Capt. J. T. 9
, Capt. John W. 2, 53
, Josephine 2
, Louisa Ann 84
, Margaret Scott 2
, Martha E. 10
, Martha T. 6
, M. T. 5
, Mary E. 53
, Mary Va. 32
, O. E. 5
, Paul Bradford 109
, Rebecca Frances 53
, Robert E. 36
, Sally S. 53
, Robert E. 36
, Sally S. 53
, S. A. 53
, S. C. 53
, S. J. 53
, S. L. 53
, Sam 109
, Susan J. 53
, Susan R. 10
, Tennie Barnett 109
, William 53
, Wm. R. T. 5
, Wright W. 53
Snedecor, Anne Blake 53
, Eleanor 52
, F. P. 53
, Col. James 51, 52
, L. C. 53
, Sallie S. 52
Snoddy, Elizabeth 61
, Dr. Levert 61
, Mamie Lois 108
, Mary Alice 61
, Dr. Sam 61
, Dr. Virgil 61
Sorshy, Stephen 27
, W. C. 27
Soule, John M. 84, 85
Sparkman, John Lee 109
Speed, Benjamin 5

Speed, J. B. 5
, James B. 4
, James F. 3
, James T. 3
, Jonnie 3
, Lizzie 5
, M. S. 5
, Mary 3
, William Alexander 66
Speight, Annie 93
, Edward 95
, Edward G. 95
, James F. 95
, Martha E. 95
, Mary 95
, Seth 95
Spencer, Florence Lamb 9
, Helen Neville Grant 113
, Robert S. Neville 113
, Sara H. 112, 113
, Wm. Hervey Jr. 113
Spidle, Elizabeth 4
, Frances 4
, Harry L. 4
, Jacob 4
, Jake 3
, John M. 3, 22
, Mary 22
, Robert 4
, Sallie E. 3
Spivey, G. B. 92
, Geo. 86, 92
Spraggins, Wm. 64
Stalworth, Charles D. 20
, Sahra 20
, William W. 20, 24
Stallworth, Elizabeth 33
, John 33
, Sara 33
Stapp, Winifred 42
Stark, Martha Jane 49
Stancel, Mary Lou 43
, Riddle Jane 43
, Rev. W. R. 43
, Dr. W. R. 43
, Wm. B. 43
Stanton, E. J. 47
, Eugene 47
, H. L. 47
, Henry G. 47
, J. Condre 95
, Mary Eugenia 47

Stuart, R. F. 11
    , Dr. Robert F. 84
    , W. C. 107
    , Wannie Louise 109
    , W. H. 109
Sturdivant, Martha A.
Sulzby, Clara J. 76
    , Ida T. 30
    , James P. 75
    , Philip P. 75
Summerville, G. W. 61
      , Mary E. 61
Swoop, Sidney 83
Taggart, Drucilla 110
    , Mary 110
    , Wm. 110
Tarr, Carrie Lee 24
    , Frank B. 33
    , F. B. 24
    , R. L. 24, 33
Taulmin, Harry 36
Taylor, A. M. 109
    , C. J. 81
    , Dock Mills 5
    , Edward Erie 94
    , Eliza Amason 94
    , Eliza Ashley Todd 32
    , Elizabeth 81
    , Ella May 94
    , Frances 42
    , Francis 92
    , Ida Lamb 9
    , James B. 42
    , James Oscar 104
    , J. Matt 9
    , John J. 42
    , J. R. 32
    , M. E. 32
    , Mary 81
    , Madison B. 5
    , Mary Ella Barnes 32
    , Meredith 42
    , Minnie M. 109
    , Octavia L. 5
    , Samuel 31
    , Dr. Samuel Wm. 94
    , Thomas 42
    , Thomas H. 42
    , Thomas W. 32
    , Dr. Thompson W. 35
    , Travis 30
    , Ullman 104

    , W. F. 97
    , Walter G. 104
    , W. S. 31
    , Wm. White 94
    , Zealous 81
Thaxton, Charles Madison 98
    , Henry 68
    , Lucy Grow 68
    , Nancy Jane 98
    , Sara J. 98
    , Wm. 98
Theodore, T. T. May 92
    , Thaddens 92
Theroux, Bettie Neal 96
    , Frank Archie 96
Thetford, Samuel M. D. 17
Thigpen, Sophie L. 94
Thomas, Eleanor 49
    , J. A. 102
    , J. B. 102
    , Martha A. 98
    , M. E. 102
    , T. J. 102
    , Virginia Anderson 24
    , Alexander 12, 24
    , E. X. 30
Thompson, Geo, R. 102
    , John 23
    , Joshua R. 102
    , Mary 14
    , Nancy M. 102
    , Sara A. 30
    , Clara Neal 29
Thornton, Elisha 10
    , Frances 74
    , Col. J. I. 8
    , James 10
    , Luke 10
    , Mary 29
    , Nancy C. 10
    , Sam Snoddy 29
    , W. P. 74
    , W. R. 29
Thurmond, Ann E. 105
    , Fielding L. 105
    , Franklin 105
    , T. R. 105
Tilman, Annie W. 52
    , D. W. 13
    , Daniel W. 52
    , Mary H. 13
    , Melissa 13

Weaver, Elizabeth 101
        , James M. 101
        , William 81
Webb, Col. J. D. 50
    , Va. Jarvis 38
Webster, Bettie 77
        , D. T. 77
        , Rev. J. R. 24
Wedgworth, Esther 78
            , James 78
            , Dr. Middleton 78
Wells, B. Barlow 76
Weston, A. G. 97
        , Wlizabeth 45
        , G. L. 97
        , Mary 45
        , Robert 45
        , Wm. K. 96
Whelan, Adeline 48
        , Charles 48
        , Helen 49
White, Andrew T. 62
    , Asa 104
    , Capt. Asa 33
    , Ben 94
    , C. C. 104
    , David 74
    , E. F. 62
    , Harveys 14
    , Hugh L. 33
    , James W. 64
    , Janie 64, 74
    , Jennie 74
    , John 14
    , John S. 62
    , Laura A. E. 14
    , Martha 74
    , Martha Dirrut 12
    , Martha D. 94
    , Mary 101
    , Mattie Monee 74
    , Miriam E. 94
    , Moses 75
    ., P. M. 74
    , Sam 101
    , Sara 101
    , S. M. 74
    , Thos. W. 62
    , W. B. 104
    , William A. 74

Whitfield, John W. 56
            , Mary E. Seale 56
Whitehead, Albert Pinckney 27
            , Jajor E. D. 27
            , Rebecca 27
Whitsett, James T. 105
        , Kizzah 69
Whitten, Wm. W. 82
Whittle, Nettie M. Aust 106
Wiggins, A. A. 109
        , Claude C. 109
        , M. E. 109
        , Oscar Irving 109
        , T. F. 109
Wilburn, Wm. Clarence 57
Wilbourn, T. H. 101
Wilburn, Essie Phillips 27
        , William Clarence 27
Wilder, Nancy 100
        , Green 100
Wiley, James Edward 49
        , Jajor James Heratio 49
        , Josephine Bayool 49
        , Julius 49
        , Frances 11
        , Mary 11
Wilkins, Dr. A. M. 101
        , John E. 101
        , Nancy 68
        , Rev. Richard 68
Wilkinson S. 47
William, C. 98
        , Clarence 11
        , C. W. 81
        , David H. M. D. 11
Williams, Eli 35
        , Elizabeth 91
        , Eugenia Floride 11
        , Fannie 90
        , Greshal 29
        , H. L. 101
        , Dr. Henry L. 64
        , Huldah 29
        , Maggie J. 35
        , Maria 50
        , Mary 81
        , O. 81
        , Rianna E. 29
        , Thomas Hopkins 101
        , V. P. 101
        , Wheaton 90

Williamson, James 84
        , Lena Harris 85
        , Lucy 34
Williamson, Susan D. 84
        , Virginia B. 84
Willima, Philander 91
Wills, E.. M. 14
        , James 15
        , Wm. B. 14
Wilmouth, Nancy 15
Wilson, Cephas Love 21
        , David 26
        , Della Mariah 21, 22
        , Elizabeth K. 25
        , Emily Beverly 21
        , James Ezra 25, 34
        , Jesse F. 56
        , John A. 77
        , Dr. John Calvin 26
        , J. D. 56
        , John Walter 57
        , Lavinia Jordan 21
        , Lewis G. 26
        , Mary E. 25
        , Mary Selma 26
        , Norma 2
        , Pennie F. 57
        , Robert B. 21
        , Robert Bullington 22
        , Romania 78
        , Samuel A. 25
        , Samuel J.
        , Sara 25
        , Sara Florella 26
        , Susan A. Jones 26
        , Wm. M. 25
Wimberly, Andrew Jackson 6
        , Cora Landrum 6
        , Ernest Joel 6
Windorn, Sara 81
        , William 81
Windham, Betty W. 96

Windham, James 45
        , James Irvin 96
        , J. S. 45
        , Lula B. 45
        , Mattie 45
Wimm, Frank 25
        , L. W. 25
        , M. J. 25
        , Thos. F. 35
        , Va. Brown 32, 35
Winston, Capt. Anthony 39
        , Col. John A. 34, 39
        , Capt. John James 34
        , Col. John M. 36
Winston, John Milton 36
        , Lucy N. 36
Wiyzer, Capt. Jacob 31
Wocke, W. L. 107
Wood, Mattie J. 62
        , William H. 53
Woodall, Candice A. 62
        , Elizabeth 62
        , Elizabeth J. 62
        , Emeline C. 62
        , James 62
        , John 62
        , Mary M. 62
Woodson, Christina Herndon 84
        , Lucie C. 84
        , Reavis B. 84
Wyatt, Betty 50
        , Dr. R. R. 101
Wynn, Osmun Appling 77
        , Erasmus 77
        , Jane 77
        , Williamson Robert 77
Young, Ottis 97
Youngblood, Mittie Bradford 64